PORTLAND

A PUBLICATION OF
GREATER PORTLAND LANDMARKS
INCORPORATED

*"Entertainment of the Boston Rifle Rangers by the
Portland Riflle Club in 1829" by Charles Codman*

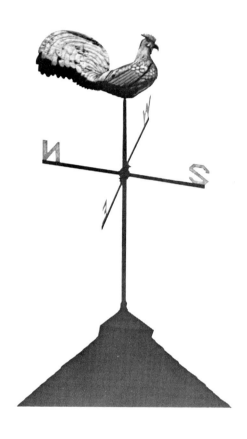

Weathervane, 57 Exchange Street

Designer and Editor	MARTIN DIBNER
Photography	NICHOLAS DEAN
Architecture Text	PATRICIA McGRAW PANCOAST
History Text	JOSEPHINE H. DETMER
Project Director	JANE SMITH MOODY

4

FOREWORD   7

INTRODUCTION   11

HISTORY

    Settlement to Statehood   17

    Statehood to Disaster   39

    From the Ashes   75

ARCHITECTURE

    Late Colonial and Federal Styles   97

    Revival Styles   131

    Victorian Portland   169

LOST BUILDINGS   223

GLOSSARY   226

ACKNOWLEDGMENTS   232

CREDITS   233

STREET GUIDE TO BUILDINGS   234

FOREWORD

During the last decade an increasing number of fine old Portland buildings and neighborhoods have been demolished to make space for modern developments. Some destruction is, of course, inevitable if we are to keep pace with the economic growth of the city. All too often, however, Portland has experienced indiscriminate and wholesale razing which has irreparably damaged the traditional look of our urban environment.

The formation of Greater Portland Landmarks in the early 1960's reflected a growing awareness that one of the most effective means for combating this wanton destruction is through educational programs designed to help the public understand and appreciate the value of Portland's historic architecture. The struggle is far from over; each year witnesses the passing of still more fine buildings. Yet the idea of progress through preservation is beginning to take hold; hopefully, enough of our older buildings, streetscapes, and neighborhoods may be saved to retain the city's historic character.

Opposite: 384 Cumberland Avenue
Both structures demolished 1963

7

An essential part of Landmarks' education program has been a building-by-building, street-by-street inventory which is still underway. This survey prompted the idea of preparing and publishing a guide to and a history of the city's notable buildings and streets. The peninsula, the site of Portland's original settlement, provides a manageable geographical entity and it is hoped that other areas of the city may be given similar attention in the future. Individual buildings were chosen on the basis of architectural excellence, historical interest, and typicalness of period, style and use. Attention was also given to the location of particular buildings as a focal point for an entire area.

Portland City Hall, a notable success aesthetically and functionally, is the latest of the buildings chosen for inclusion in the book. This does not mean that Landmarks is not interested in modern architecture. Indeed, Landmarks is vitally concerned with the new and in its ability, in contemporary terms, to live up to, enhance, and in turn be enhanced by the best of the old.

This book is an expression of Landmarks' philosophy that the best of the past must be preserved as a living part of the present. Only a few of the buildings included in these pages are museums. Most are being used as homes and business establishments while serving as a permanent inspiration and reminder of Portland's proud history and the timeless beauty of her architectural heritage.

CHARLTON S. SMITH

President

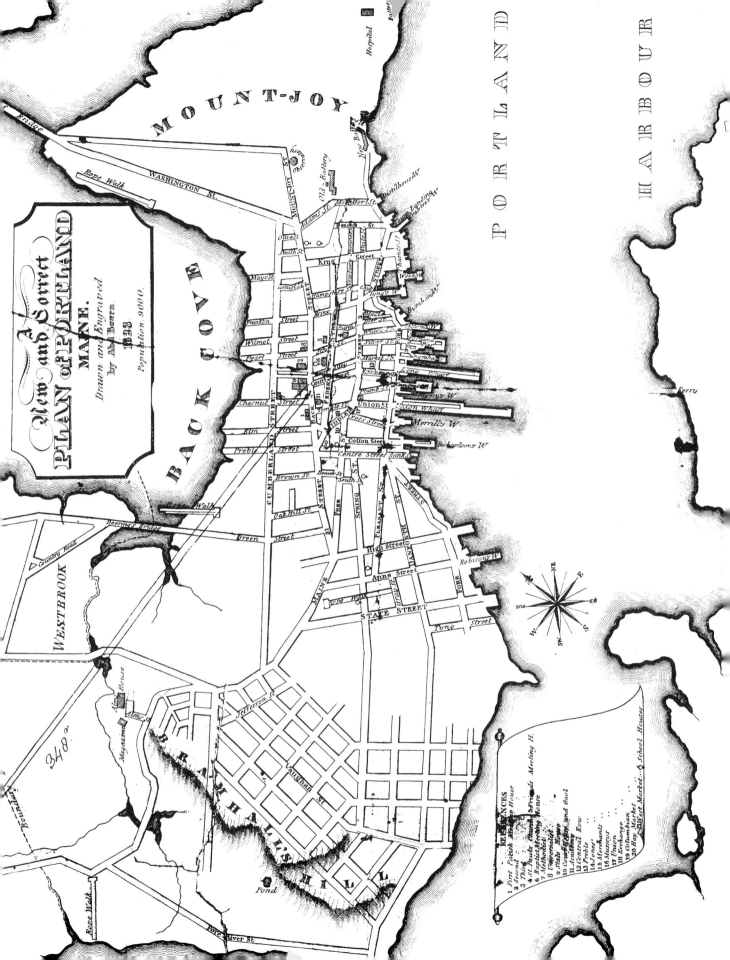

INTRODUCTION

The water-ringed peninsula on which Portland stands suggests a gigantic double-ended Viking ship about to put to sea. It is long and narrow — nearly three miles by an average width of about three quarters of a mile — with Munjoy Hill rising 160 feet above the sea as its prow and Bramhall Hill, fifteen feet higher, as its stern. From the central ridge that connects these two eminences the land slopes down to Portland Harbor on the south and to Back Cove on the north. One has, in consequence, a pleasing view of some kind from many points on the peninsula. The earliest settlement was, of course, by the harbor. At the outbreak of the American Revolution the town had only three streets of any great length: Fore Street running along the waterfront, and inland Middle and Back Streets, which converged to form today's Congress Street which was the principal route to the mainland. By 1823, when Abel Bowen's map was engraved, the town extended over the central ridge from the harbor to the cove, but the hills were still open country, as they substantially remained until the middle of the nineteenth century. Indeed the Portland Observatory, rising 222 feet above tidewater, which was built in 1807 to give timely warning of approaching vessels, was long isolated on Munjoy Hill. In the course of the nineteenth century the city covered the entire peninsula, but with a proper respect for the natural features of the landscape, for the hills at the prow and stern were converted into sightly Eastern and Western Promenades, while Deering's Oaks, a fifty acre tract near the Back Cove with fine trees, was set aside as a public park.

Architecturally Portland is predominantly a nineteenth century city, built in the days of its greatest prosperity as a seaport and railroad center. It has a human scale and a pleasing variety, for the contours of the peninsula and the varied street pattern not only provide delightful views in many directions but break the city up into manageable units. It is blessedly free of the monotony of Manhattan Island or of cities set in a boundless prairie. The waterfront, the business district, and residential regions have their own distinct characters, yet all Portland areas are close together and blend into each other without abrupt transitions. In looking at the city, one thinks not so much of isolated buildings of superlative quality, but of harmonious neighborhoods and streetscapes that have preserved enough of their original character to warrant respect.

Many American cities in the past quarter century have denatured themselves by groveling obeisance to the automobile. My impression of many comes down to a few fine buildings, rising like islands from a sea of highways, parking lots, and displays of used cars being offered for sale. Portland thus far has been more discreet. I have come to the city on and off for thirty-five years, and can still wander through its streets with pleasure. Middle Street is, of course, poorer without the great mass of the Falmouth Hotel and the marble Post Office that dignified the corner of Exchange Street, but enough of its nineteenth century commercial character remains to deserve serious consideration as something that makes Portland different from

12

other cities. Most Americans take their surroundings for granted without considering what makes them attractive or ugly. Only when some radical change occurs do they begin to think about elements in the cityscape or landscape. As I have for some years been trying to explain to my neighbors the significance that certain buildings and regions have for the character of Boston, I am happy that Greater Portland Landmarks has prepared this book, which should do much to make residents of Portland aware of their surroundings.

A building does not have to be of great antiquity to be pleasing or have architectural quality. A region does not have to contain buildings of a single age or style to be agreeable. Good buildings of any period fit with their neighbors, provided their scale, mass, and materials are harmonious. The very diversity of architectural styles that exists in some parts of Portland helps to make the city the pleasant place that it is. I hope that this book will make residents of Portland look at their scene with greater intelligence and appreciation and inspire them to find good uses for certain meritorious buildings that have temporarily fallen on evil days.

Most buildings can be preserved only if they are kept in current use as part of daily life. Throughout the United States there are already more "historic house museums" open for exhibition than we can afford as a nation or that make any sense. Good buildings should be used rather than shown off like a butterfly impaled on a pin. Professional men can practice law or medicine or fill teeth quite as well in a handsome old building as in a jerry-built new one. Banks, gas companies, and any number of businesses can have their offices in structures originally built for other uses. It is simply a matter of having the imagination to see how it can be done. Charleston, South Carolina, has shown the way in many instances. In Boston the old City Hall of the 1860's — a fine example of the architectural influence of the French Second Empire — has just been converted to business use. A bank, a first rate restaurant, an insurance agency and some firms of lawyers have found its well proportioned rooms more attractive for their purposes than space in new skyscrapers. Houses too large for the servantless present day can often be converted into apartments, offices, clubs, or other institutions. It should be the first rule of preservation to try to find some good contemporary use for any building whose architectural quality is outstanding, or that is a harmonious neighbor to important buildings in the region.

Obviously not all activities of the present day can be accommodated in renovated old buildings. Nor should new buildings be gargantuanly enlarged approximations of old ones. In building a fire house or a supermarket it is patently absurd to add a cupola copied from Independence Hall in Philadelphia. The important thing is that the quality of their design be as good as that of their older neighbors, and that their scale and materials not be wilfully disharmonious with whatever prevails in the region where they are placed. Change for its own sake is not progress, but carefully considered change can enhance the existing good qualities of a city. Portland in 1972 has a distinctive character of its own. I hope that it always will. The surest way of achieving that is to have its residents become aware of the significance of their surroundings; it is to that end that this book is designed.

WALTER MUIR WHITEHILL
Director,
Boston Athenaeum

14

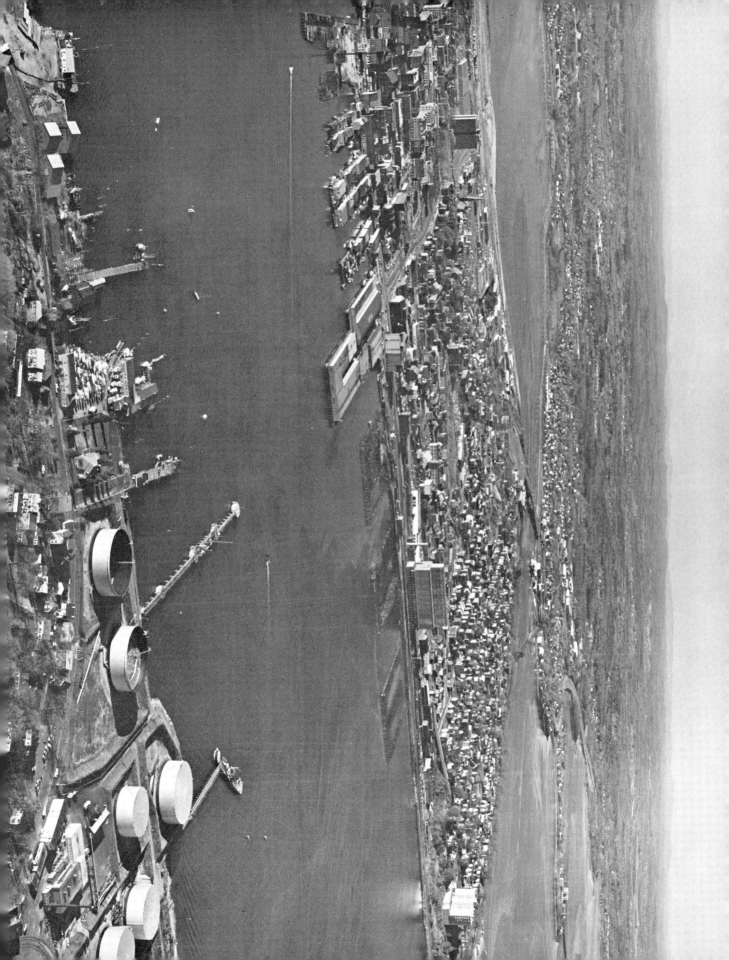

HISTORY

1628-1820

SETTLEMENT TO STATEHOOD

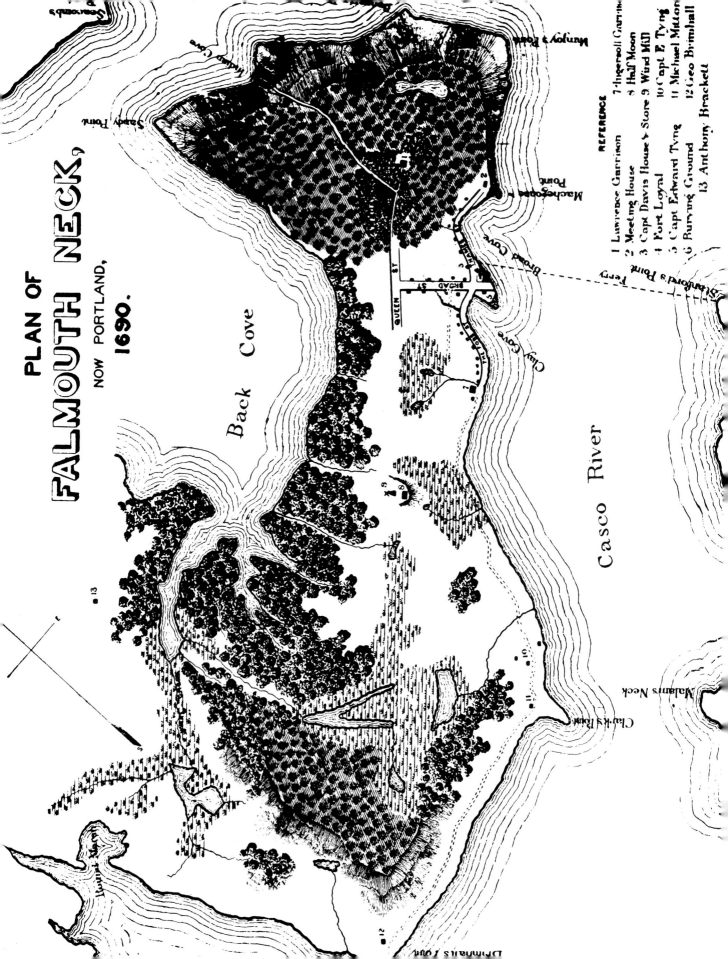

PLAN OF FALMOUTH NECK,

NOW PORTLAND, 1690.

Back Cove

Casco River

Saudy Point

Mackegaue Point

Munjoy Point

Sandford's Point

Ferry

Broad Cove

Clay Cove

QUEEN ST

BROAD ST

FORE ST

Adams Neck

Clark's Point

Round Marsh

Brimar's Point

REFERENCE

1 Lawrence Garrison
2 Meeting House
3 Capt Davis House & Store
4 Fort Loyal
5 Capt Edward Tyng
6 Burying Ground
7 Ingersoll Garrison
8 Half Moon
9 Wind Mill
10 Capt E. Tyng
11 Michael Mitton
12 Geo Bramhall
13 Anthony Brackett

THE BEGINNINGS

Portland has a gallant history. It has endured devastating Indian attacks, bombardment, and catastrophic storm and fire. Time after time, Portlanders have had to rebuild their ruined homes and start anew. The indomitable will to survive has characterized Portland and her people since its troubled beginnings.

The distinction of being the first permanent settler in the Portland area goes to Walter Bagnall. In 1628 he set up a trading post on Richmond Island. His claim to fame was brief, however, because in 1631 he was murdered by Indians he had cheated. John Winter, the agent of Plymouth merchants, was the next settler on Richmond Island. He developed a flourishing trade in fish and furs.

Since Winter would not allow Richard Tucker and George Cleeves to settle at the mouth of the Spurwink River opposite thriving Richmond Island, they turned to Machigonne, as the Indians called the neck of land which projected into Casco Bay.

19

They built Portland's first crude house on the corner of what is now Hancock and Fore Streets in 1632. They too tried to develop trade in fish and furs with the Indians, and in 1637 Sir Fernando Gorges, the Proprietor of Maine, granted them a deed to the land on Casco Neck.

As time passed, other families migrated to the area. Among the early settlers were George Munjoy, after whom Munjoy Hill is named, and Richard Martin, who settled at the mouth of the Presumpscot. Martin's Point bears his name. In 1658 Massachusetts commissioners declared the area "formerly called Spurwink and Casco Bay from the east of Spurwink River, to the Clapboard islands, in Casco bay, shall run back eight miles in the country, and henceforth shall be called by the name of Falmouth." Early Falmouth included present-day Portland, South Portland, Falmouth, Cape Elizabeth and Westbrook. Falmouth derived its name from an ancient Cornwall town at the mouth of the Fal River, whence came several early English settlers.

Enterprising people moved to Falmouth. Mills were set up at Capisic and the lower falls of the Presumpscot River. By 1675 forty families had settled in Falmouth. Their houses were scattered over a large area.

The Puritans in Massachusetts took over the Province of Maine, and in 1669 the Massachusetts Court ordered Falmouth to engage a Congregational minister. Although Robert Jordan, who had married Winter's daughter and settled on Richmond Island, was an Anglican priest, this did not satisfy the Massachusetts zealots. George Burroughs became the first Congregational minister. He was reportedly a very strong man, able to pick up a barrel with his hooked thumb. During the Salem witch hunt in later years, his strength was said to be "derived from the Prince of Evil." On the questionable evidence of a twelve-year old child, among others, he was tried and hung for witchcraft.

Until 1675 Falmouth's relations with the Indians seem to have been peaceful enough, but in that year King Philip, sachem of the Wampanoag tribe, fed up with wrongs inflicted

King Philip

on his people by the colonists, went on the war path. It was the beginning of a period of terrible conflict with the French and the Indians. The power struggle between England and France was fought in Maine as well as all over the globe. For the next century Maine was the arena for some of the bloodiest battles of the Colonial period because she was located strategically between French Canada and her Indian allies and the other English colonies. In 1676, thirty-four Falmouth inhabitants were killed or captured. All those who escaped the tomahawk fled their homes. Others led by Burroughs escaped to Cushing's Island where they waited ten days to be rescued. Homes in Falmouth were burned and destroyed. Desolation spread over the countryside.

A peace was made in 1678 and the survivors began to return to their ruined homes. Governor Thomas Danforth ordered the people resettled in a more compact manner so it would be easier to resist future Indian attacks. In 1680 Fort Loyall was built at the foot of King Street (renamed India Street after the Revolution). Grants were made around the fort in every direction to both new and old settlers. Soon a village had sprung up and the community prospered.

Captain Sylvanus Davis ran a sawmill and was licensed to retail liquors in his store and warehouse. George Bramhall built a tannery at the foot of Bramhall Hill. The Anthony Brackett family returned to their farm (present-day Deering's Oaks). They had been captured by Indians and during the march to Canada resourceful Mrs. Brackett had spotted a canoe. She sewed up its ripped seams and her family was able to escape and paddle to safety. Richard Seacomb had built the first "ordinary" (public house) near the foot of King Street. By the time the Second Indian War erupted in 1688, there were six or seven hundred people settled in Falmouth.

In 1689, Brackett's farm was the scene of one of the fiercest Indian battles of the French and Indian wars. Fortunately for the Falmouth settlers, Major Benjamin Church, a professional Indian fighter, arrived with his forces from Massachusetts at the same time a war party of seven hundred Indians converged on Casco Bay. On September 21st, the Indians were engaged in Brackett's orchard. The fighting raged over six hours until the Indians were forced to retreat into the forests. Falmouth was saved but Church had to leave, and the people spent an anxious winter wondering when and where the Indians would strike next.

The following spring the Indians went on the warpath again and Falmouth was completely annihilated. On May 15th, a party of thirty men, suspecting the Indians to be in the area, scouted up Munjoy Hill and were ambushed. Fourteen were killed. The rest fled to the nearby garrison and then under cover of night to Fort Loyall. The Indians burned dwellings and laid siege to the fort where all the inhabitants had gathered. Fort Loyall was on an overhanging bluff and the enemy could easily harass the fort out of reach of its guns. Captain Sylvanus Davis, commander of the fort, who was taken prisoner to Quebec and survived, later reported, "They fought us five days and four nights, in which time they killed and wounded the greatest part of our men, burned all the houses, and at last we were forced to parley with them . . ." The French promised the besieged good quarter but went back on their word and allowed the Indians to scalp and slaughter with a vengeance. The dead were not buried until two years later when Sir William Phipps and Major Church came upon the scene of horror. There were no white settlers left alive in Maine east of Wells. Peace was finally made again in 1699, but as Portland historian William Willis later reported, Falmouth was a perfect blank, a thoroughfare for the savage and a resort for beasts of prey.

EARLY GROWTH

Settlers began straggling back to Falmouth. In 1715 only one family lived on the Neck, but by 1718 twenty families had moved into the area. When the Reverend Thomas Smith (whose diary is an invaluable source of information about old Falmouth from 1725 to 1788) became the permanent preacher

The Reverend Thomas Smith

22

of the First Parish in 1727, he reported about forty families clustered around the lower part of King Street, "some of which were respectable." For some of the old settlers it was their third attempt at making Falmouth their home. New settlers were encouraged to come to Falmouth, and in 1727 the town voted to admit inhabitants who could share the common land by paying ten pounds to the impoverished town treasury. The town gained 138 people and Parson Smith notes: "a spring was thus given to the increase and prosperity of the town, by the enterprise of the new settlers."

Falmouth did not suffer during the Third Indian War because troops were headquartered here. In 1727 Munjoy Hill was the scene of an important and colorful powwow with the Indians. The Governor of Massachusetts and over two hundred Indians held a conference in a tremendous tent specially set up for the occasion. A public dinner celebrated the new peace. General Wolfe's heroic capture of Quebec in 1759 completely broke the power of the French and deprived the Indians of allies. The English colonists who had suffered so much had reason to rejoice. Parson Smith reports in his diary, "The country is all in ecstasy upon the surprising news of the conquest of Quebec." Well it might be, for a century of Indian warfare had ended.

When Parson Smith came to Falmouth, the three principal streets extending westerly from King Street were the Fore, the Middle, and the Back (later known as Queen and now as Congress Street). The meeting house was on the corner of Middle and King Streets. In 1740 when a new one, fondly called "Old Jerusalem," was built on the present Congress Street site, its location was considered far out in the country. There was no house on the Neck north of Back Street and forest and swamp covered most of the land west to Bramhall Hill. The business of the town, lumbering and fishing, was done around the foot of King Street and the beach below, which had the town landing.

Besides paying him seventy pounds a year and supplying

him with farm produce, Parson Smith's parishioners built him a fine house. It had the only wallpapered room in town. The paper was put on with nails and the room was referred to proudly as "the papered room." Church attendance was compulsory. Winter Sundays were something of an endurance test; the church was unheated and the baptism water, as well as the parishioners' feet, often froze. In addition to his responsibilities for Sunday's prayers and lengthy sermons, Parson Smith tended to his flock's medical needs. Life was not easy, and there was a great deal of sickness. The year 1737 seems to have been a particularly hard one with seventy-five people dying of "throat distemper."

In the years before the American Revolution, Falmouth's population and wealth greatly increased. With the best natural harbor on the eastern seaboard (its deep channel is sheltered by islands and near the open ocean), Falmouth became a bustling maritime center. Lumber was the basis of prosperity. Mills were set up at the mouths of rivers. By 1752 there were ten saw and grist mills operating in the First Parish. In 1765 Parson Smith wrote in his diary, "The ships and other vessels loading here are a wonderful benefit to us. They take off vast quantities of timber, masts, oak rafters, boards, etc."

In 1727 Thomas Westbrook, Royal Mast Agent, had moved here and Falmouth became a supplier of the giant pines for the British Royal Navy. The tallest trees were marked with the broad arrow and shipped to England in specially-built mast ships. Between 1768 and 1772 Falmouth shipped out 1,046 masts to England, averaging over three tons apiece.

In addition to masts, Falmouth shipped planks, boards and timbers to England in return for necessities such as scissors, pots and kettles, and bolts of cloth. Lumber and staves for barrels, as well as salted fish, were shipped to the West Indies in exchange for cargoes of rum and other West Indian goods. Cord wood and planks went to Boston and other colonies in exchange for agricultural goods.

Lumbering was so profitable that the people neglected agriculture. They were dependent on commerce to supply their

Opposite page: "Old Jerusalem," meeting house of the First Parish, 1740-1825

24

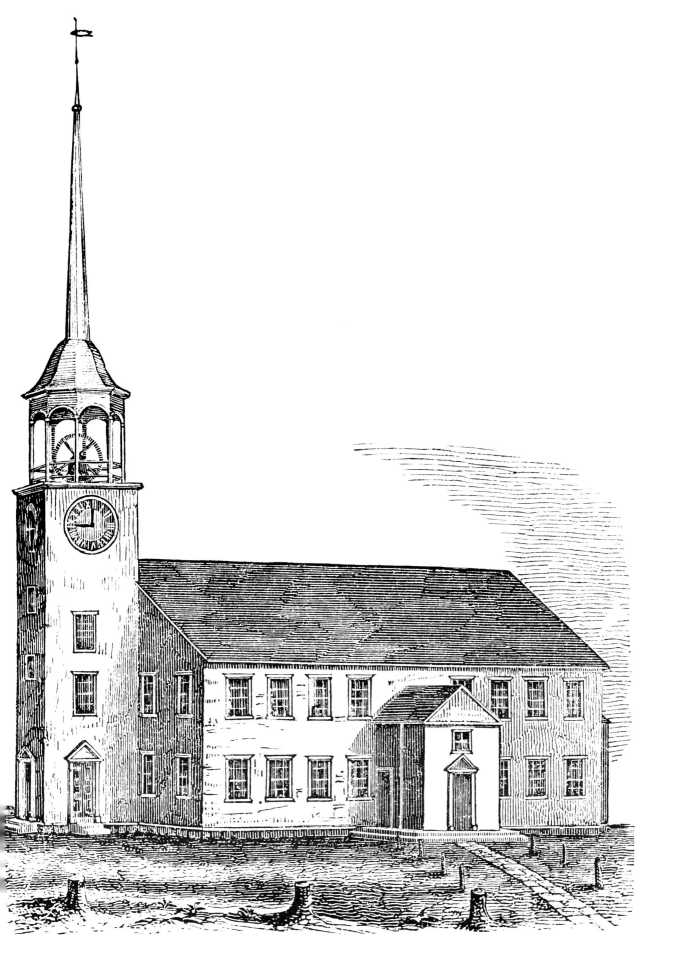

basic necessities. Parson Smith reports March 5, 1737, "All the talk is, — no corn, no hay and there is not a peck of potatoes to eat in all the eastern country." In late winter and early spring, merchants could count on an excellent market for food supplies.

In addition to lumbering and fishing, Falmouth also began building ships. Sometimes merchants would build their ships, fill them with fish or lumber and when they reached port sell both ship and cargo. Falmouth's early merchants seem to have been an enterprising group. Men like Enoch Freeman, Ephraim Jones, Samuel Moody and the Waite brothers, all who had customers and suppliers from Halifax to Barbados, took advantage of both Falmouth's natural resources and any trade opportunity. They prospered and so did their town by the sea.

TROUBLES WITH ENGLAND

The American Revolution temporarily ended Falmouth's prosperous growth. Troubles with England started in 1764. To pay for the French and Indian wars, England tried to raise money in the colonies by enforcing her Navigation Acts. She passed the Sugar Act, which Falmouth merchants flouted by smuggling their West Indian molasses into port without paying a duty. In 1765 when Parliament passed the Stamp Act, Falmouth courts did business without the stamps. An aroused mob, after a parade through town, threatened the tax collectors and burned the stamps. When the hated act was repealed, Smith reported, "Our people are mad with drink and joy; bells ringing, drums beating, colors flying, the courthouse illuminated and some others, and a bonfire, and a deluge of drunkenness."

A Committee of Correspondence was chosen to communicate with the other colonies. The town reported itself opposed to the English Parliament taxing the colonies to raise revenue and heartily endorsed the theory of no taxation without representation. "Neither the Parliament of Great Britain nor any other power on earth has a right to lay a tax on us but by our

Spitfire Bomb.

Cat .

26

own consent or the consent of those whom we may choose to represent us."

Falmouth applauded the Boston Tea Party and stopped using tea. England retaliated by closing the port of Boston. Falmouth was in complete sympathy with the Boston patriots. Smith reported that a muffled bell tolled all day without cessation and a day of fast was held on account of the gloomy state of affairs. When news of Lexington and Concord reached Falmouth, the town immediately voted to raise a company of sixty men and dispatched them to join the fight.

Now committed on the side of the colonists, Falmouth's involvement almost immediately became more serious and led to her third destruction. It began with a shipment of masts.

Early in 1775, Captain Thomas Coulson, a local Tory, launched a thousand-ton mast ship. The town refused to allow him to complete the outfitting of the ship with sails, rigging and stores which had come from England. Coulson successfully enlisted the aid of a British sloop of war, Captain Henry Mowatt commanding. Later in May of that year, fired by the events at Lexington, a small group of unruly patriots captured Captain Mowatt while he was on a hunting expedition and held him for a brief time. In June Captain Coulson again angered the patriots by trying to dispatch a load of masts to England. He was thwarted again. The masts never did become masts for the Royal Navy but were hidden up the Fore River and years later, in 1835, became the underpinnings of Sawyer's Wharf at the foot of High Street.

Store Vessel.

Falmouth paid a heavy price for pulling the British lion's tail. The following October Mowatt returned with four armed vessels and orders to execute a just punishment on the town. His terms were harsh. The town would be spared only if all cannon and small arms were handed over to the British by the next morning. Although they knew it meant the destruction of their homes and property, the Falmouth inhabitants defiantly voted to reject the British terms.

At nine o'clock Mowatt opened fire on the exposed town.

27

Canceau

THE TOWN of FALMOUTH,

People fled for their lives. Although many had been moving their belongings to safety all night, pandemonium reigned as families were separated and possessions scattered in the rush for safety. The furious bombardment lasted twelve hours. About one hundred British seamen landed and set fires throughout the town. Four hundred fourteen of the town's five hundred buildings were destroyed. Falmouth lay in ashes. To add to the misery, it rained the next three days. Parson Smith's son wept when he saw the ruins. Winter was approaching and on every quarter poverty and desolation met the unhappy sufferers.

28

rnt, by Captain MOET, O_{ctb}: 18th 1775.

Many had to leave Falmouth because their homes were demolished. For a long time provisions were scarce. Parson Smith reports that a barrel of flour cost him a whole year's salary.

In spite of their hardships, Falmouth pledged that the town would solemnly engage with their lives and fortunes to support Congress. They sent many men to fight with the Continental Army and were commended by the Massachusetts General Court for being foremost in furnishing their quota. William Willis records: "Few towns felt more ardently, and none suffered more severely in the cause of independence, than Falmouth."

29

INDEPENDENCE AND GROWTH

After the War for Independence, on July 4, 1786, the Neck separated from the rest of Falmouth. It was decided to name the newly created town Portland. Cushing's (or Bang's) Island had at one time been called Portland and the head of land opposite had always been called Portland Head with the water between called Portland Sound. Though Portland had a population of almost two thousand, it was smaller than York, Falmouth or Gorham. The new town was still struggling to regain a measure of the prosperity she had enjoyed before Mowatt's bombardment. Parson Smith laments on May 2, 1787, "Hard times! No money! No business!"

The town by the sea began a period of unparalleled growth. By 1792 Portland had erected 234 new buildings. In 1800 the population had grown to 3,704 and by 1820 it had reached 8,581. In 1797 Dr. Timothy Dwight, President of Yale, could say of Portland, "No American town is more entirely commercial and of course none is more sprightly." On another trip in 1807 he commented, "Few towns in New England are equally beautiful and brilliant. Its wealth and business are probably quadrupled."

Men of ability and perseverance carved out fortunes for themselves and helped Portland prosper. Nathaniel Deering opened the first store on Fore Street after Mowatt's bombardment and helped build Long Wharf at the foot of Fish (now

View of Portland, 1786

Exchange) Street. He was prudent, industrious and had considerable good luck.

A man Portland should remember with gratitude is Joseph H. Ingraham. Parson Smith describes him as a man of great enterprise and public spirit. When he built his silversmith's shop on Fore Street in 1777 it was considered a rash undertaking in the exposed state of the town. Later he opened up Market Street from Middle to Fore and built a large portion of Commercial Wharf, which formerly bore his name. He was also responsible for developing State Street, called one of the grandest and most enterprising schemes in our town's history. He obtained the land, which the government had confiscated from the Toryist Tyng family and built the first house on State Street in 1801. For a while Portland's largest landholder, Ingraham sold off lots to such prominent people as Colonel Richard Hunnewell, County Sheriff; and Prentiss Mellen, the Federalist Senator from Massachusetts and later Maine's first Chief Justice. State Street became the handsomest avenue of private residences in the city.

William Vaughan was another post-Revolutionary visionary. He anticipated Portland's expansion westward and bought about four hundred acres of land on Bramhall Hill. He instigated the building of Vaughan's Bridge in 1800. Although most of Vaughan's plans for the area did not really materialize until a half century later when John B. Brown moved there, he should be given credit for his unusual foresight.

31

It was the sea, however, that made Portland thrive and brought her both fame and fortune. Shipbuilders, lumbermen, merchants and fishermen all relied on the sea. Men like Edward Oxnard and Stephen and Hugh McLellan (who became the president of Portland's first bank, which opened in 1799) made fortunes as shippers and merchants. Asa Clapp with his fleet of ships was Portland's wealthiest and most diversified merchant. He not only traded cotton and flour with the southern states but also shipped fish, molasses and lumber to England and Germany.

Portland became a lively maritime center, shipping cargoes to all corners of the earth. In 1789 Portland handled 5,000 tons of shipping. By 1807 this had increased to 39,000 tons. In 1790 George Washington authorized funds to complete Portland Head Light. In 1807 Captain Lemuel Moody promoted the building of the Portland Observatory on the highest point on Munjoy Hill. The Observatory was a vital communications center for the seafaring town. Ships in distress could be spotted by its telescope; each shipowner had a specially colored flag flown from the tower to alert the owner that his ship was nearing port. Wives of Portland seamen watched the tower to see when their loved ones were coming home. Romance and wares from all over the world sailed into Portland harbor. Sailors of a dozen nationalities thronged the busy wharves and grog shops. The waterfront was a bustling bawdy place. Henry Wadsworth Longfellow captured the colorful flavor of Portland's Fore Street and docks in the early 1800's:

> I remember the black wharves and the slips
> And the sea-tides tossing free;
> And Spanish sailors with bearded lips,
> And the beauty and mystery of the ships,
> And the magic of the sea.

In 1803 a Portland-born Navy officer's skill and courage won the admiration of the world. Commodore Edward Preble fought and subdued the Barbary pirates off Tripoli. William Willis describes him as a man of remarkable coolness and energy of

32

character, and no less distinguished for promptness of action than soundness of judgment. Preble's example of discipline and bravery influenced a generation of naval men. He is buried in Portland's Eastern Cemetery.

The year 1807 brought Portland's commercial boom to a disastrous end. To protect neutral American ships and to stop the impressment of American seamen during the Napoleonic wars, President Jefferson recommended and Congress passed the Embargo Act. No ships were permitted to leave United States ports. The Embargo Act spelled ruin for Portland. Joseph Ingraham, William Vaughan, Woodbury Storer, the McLellan brothers, John Taber and his sons (their Quaker honesty was such that "Taber bills" were treated like bank currency) all lost their fortunes. The Portland Bank failed, losing twenty-five percent of its capital stock. On December 28, 1807, the Reverend Edward Payson wrote to his father, "Such a scene of wretchedness as I have never witnessed. A large number of the most wealthy merchants have already failed, and numbers more are daily following, so that we are all threatened with universal bankruptcy." Import duties fell from $342,909 in 1806 to $41,369 in 1808. Public soup kitchens were set up. Grass grew on the once-busy wharves.

Within fourteen months the Embargo was repealed and in 1812 America again went to war with England. Portland, unlike the Federalists in the rest of Massachusetts, seems to have given the war at least luke-warm support. Its Democratic-Republican Congressman, William Widgery, openly declared, "We are told a war will be very expensive. Granted. What is money? What is all our property, compared with our honor and our liberty?"

Portland turned her energies to privateering. For a while it was her most profitable business. Ships armed and fitted at private expense sailed forth to engage and damage the enemy and to seize cargoes for their owners. The *Dash,* built by the Porter brothers, prominent Portland merchants, became the terror of the British merchant marine and the pride of Casco

Bay. The *Dart,* another privateer, on one venture captured a large shipment of rum. For years afterward "Old Dart Rum" added to the merriment of Portland get-togethers.

A tragic ending to a hard-fought sea battle marred an American victory off Monhegan Island on September 5, 1813. The British brig *Boxer* was towed into Portland harbor by the victorious *Enterprise.* Both young sea captains had died of wounds and after an impressive funeral procession were buried side by side in Eastern Cemetery. Longfellow, (really too distantly removed to have heard the battle) wrote:

> I remember the sea-fight far away,
> How it thundered o'er the tide!
> And the dead captains, as they lay
> In their graves, o'erlooking the tranquil bay,
> Where they in battle died.

Opposite: "Boxer" engages "Enterprise," 1813

The war of 1812 was a turning point in the movement to separate the District of Maine from the Commonwealth of Massachusetts. The British had taken over Castine and all of eastern Maine during the war. Maine had been desperate for help to expel the enemy but had received no assistance from politically Federalist Massachusetts. The resulting animosity added fuel to the separatist cause which had been smoldering for some time prior to the war. Portlanders Asa Clapp, Ashur Ware, William Widgery, Joshua Wingate, Jr. and their Democratic-Republican newspaper, the *Eastern Argus,* pushed strongly for separation. Several abortive attempts were made to accomplish their ends. Finally, in 1819 separation was achieved by a majority vote of 17,000 to 7,000.

A constitutional convention was held in "Old Jerusalem" in October, 1819. Although written ten years before the advent of Jacksonian Democracy, the Maine Constitution was a politically advanced document, guaranteeing religious freedom and stipulating no property qualifications for either voting or holding office.

Maine statehood became linked with the slavery question and Missouri's request for statehood. Henry Clay in an effort

Built by Daniel Davis 1794
then Clapps

CONGRES
Built by ...

to keep power in the hands of Southern senators proposed the Missouri Compromise which allowed Maine to enter the Union as a free state if Missouri was admitted as a slave state. Unfortunately, one must agree with Thomas Jefferson that the Missouri Compromise was nothing but a reprieve. He wrote to Maine's John Holmes that the Missouri question, "like a fire-bell in the night, awakened and filled me with terror."

Portland newspapers were far from unanimous in their support of the measure. The Portland *Gazette* condemned the Missouri Compromise as a scheme to perpetuate slavery. Much as it supported Maine statehood, it preferred to see the Maine Bill "sink, than bear up so wicked a freight as the slavery of Missouri." The less principled *Eastern Argus* thought that the Compromise should be supported if Maine could become a

1800.
1765
First Parish Meeting House
1740-1825

state in no other manner. Its editors, William Pitt Preble and Ashur Ware, admitted that slavery was both a moral and political evil, but "an evil too deeply seated to admit of an immediate cure. No man in his senses thinks of emancipation. All agree that it would be ruinous to master and slave."

After prolonged and heated Congressional debate, Maine was admitted to the Union on March 15, 1820. Portland served as the first capital of the new state until 1832.

Thus in 1820 the indomitable nature of the city and her people prevailed. Portland had fully recovered from past wounds and set the example for the newly formed state of Maine as a center of flourishing political and economic activity. The future, it seemed, stretched brightly ahead.

Early woodcut, State of
Maine seal, artist unknown

1820-1866

STATEHOOD TO DISASTER

THE GOLDEN YEARS

Portland grew and prospered. In 1832 when the state capital was moved to Augusta, Portland incorporated as a city. Her population had grown to over 13,000. She was a principal stage coach center, and her commercial fleet was the largest on the eastern seaboard.

In the 1830's the residential section of the city still clustered largely around the base of Munjoy Hill and the present day Lincoln Park area, with most business centered on the waterfront at Fore Street and on India and Exchange Streets. The city grew and by mid-century its character was quite changed. Business expanded along Middle Street; Commercial Street was built; and the western part of the peninsula was blossoming into a fashionable residential section.

As in pre-Revolutionary days much of the mid-nineteenth century prosperity was based on Portland's natural resources — her magnificent, sheltered harbor, the timber she exported and the fish catch from her ocean. Portland fishermen and fishing fleets caught tons of cod, mackerel, haddock and herring for export. By 1860 Maine had climbed to second place in the nation in the value of its fisheries which annually brought in over a million dollars.

The building of roads and the development of the northern and western sections of the state, enhanced Portland's significance as a port. She exported the produce of upstate and inland Maine to the markets of the world, and served as a distribution center for goods going further down east.

The 1820's and 1830's was a period of frantic canal building in the United States. With the example of New York's Erie Canal inspiring them, Portland businessmen helped finance the Cumberland and Oxford Canal linking the city with the Sebago Lake region. The Canal Bank was incorporated in 1825 and invested twenty-five percent of its capital in the new waterway. With the help of immigrant Irish laborers, construction was completed by 1830 and flatbottomed boats plied from Windham and the back country laden with lumber to be shipped from Portland.

The demands for Maine timber were heavy both at home and abroad. Before the age of steel it was the prime building material. It was needed for constructing America's mushrooming cities, for railroad ties and fuel, and to build the nation's growing merchant marine fleet.

Early in the nineteenth century the United States became the world's second largest maritime nation. One-fifth of the United States merchant marine fleet was owned by Maine businessmen. Portland men owned vessels active in the coastal trade, carrying Kennebec ice southward and shipping southern cotton to English mills. Portland ships docked all over the world. The $60,000 clipper *Portland* sailed to Bombay; Billy Gray's fast ships sailed to Russia bringing back cargoes of Russian hemp to be spun on his large Portland ropewalk.

The age of sail was Maine's golden era. Mid-nineteenth century shipyards boomed along Maine's sea coast launching

Canal steamer "Sebago" hauled out for the winter

PORTLAND, M.ᴱ 1865.

coasters, sleek and speedy clippers, and sturdy downeasters. Maine had timber handy to her building yards as well as a large and willing labor force. In 1855 Maine constructed 215,904 tons of shipping — more than one-third of the total United States production.

Portland participated in the earlier years of the shipbuilding boom with over a dozen yards in operation. Shipbuilding centered in Clay Cove before it was filled in and in the coves that nestled along Fore Street prior to the building of Commercial Street in 1852. It was probably at Lemuel Dyer's shipyard near his boyhood home on Fore Street that young Longfellow watched the fascinating activity which later inspired his poem "The Building of the Ship."

> Loud and sudden there was heard,
> All around them and below,
> The sound of hammers, blow on blow,
> Knocking away the shores and spurs.
> And see! She stirs!
> She starts, — she moves, — she seems to feel
> The thrill of life along her keel,
> And, spurning with her foot the ground,
> With one exulting, joyous bound,
> She leaps into the ocean's arms!

The lucrative West Indies trade brought immense profits to Portland. Lumber selling at eight dollars a thousand sometimes sold for as much as sixty dollars in Havana. All kinds of wood products from barrels to houseframes were shipped to the West Indies. Portland monopolized the shook trade, which consisted of manufacturing wood barrels, to be shipped knocked down, ready to be set up and nailed together when they reached the island plantations. Maine products were exchanged for molasses. Portland was a molasses port second only to New York. In 1860 six million gallons of molasses were imported. As one writer put it, "Without molasses no lumberman could be happy in the unsweetened wilderness. Pork lubricates the joints, molasses gives tenacity to the muscles." Molasses was used both as a sweetening agent and to produce rum. At one point Portland had as many as seven distilleries running night and day converting molasses into rum.

John Bundy Brown became New England's largest importer of molasses. Brown came to Portland as a fifty-dollar a year

Henry Wadsworth Longfellow
by Charles O. Cole, 1842

45

clerk in Alpheus Shaw's grocery store on Middle Street. Through perseverance and ability he became Portland's leading capitalist. He built an experimental plant in which one of his employees, Dependence H. Furbish, discovered a method of converting molasses into an excellent quality of granulated sugar. In 1855 Brown formed the Portland Sugar Company, the third sugar house to be built in the United States. It was an immense establishment with warehouses and wharves. More than two hundred and fifty barrels of sugar were produced a day. The enterprise earned over half a million dollars a year.

Brown's influence was felt throughout Portland's business community. He had interests in banking, railroads and real estate. He became the city's largest landowner. He built "Bramhall," since demolished, an imposing villa between the Western Promenade and Vaughan Street, and developed the surrounding land into the city's most beautiful residential area.

Brown's Sugar House

47

"Bramhall," J. B. Brown Residence

Other businessmen were bringing a variety of new industries to Portland. In the early 1840's after the Portsmouth railroad was built, the Portland Company manufactured steam engines and railroad equipment which it shipped all over the world. Captain John B. Coyle formed the Portland Steam Packet Company and promoted steamboat navigation in Maine. In 1852 John B. Davis successfully manufactured spruce gum which gave Portland an early monopoly in the production of chewing gum. D. White and Sons imported bristles for their famous hand-made brushes from distant Siberia.

No man showed greater vision or determination than John A. Poor. He was responsible for Portland becoming the terminus of the Atlantic & St. Lawrence Railroad. In an era when shipbuilding was at its peak and Maine clipper ships were setting records to California and bringing prosperity to coastal towns, Poor understood that railroads held the key to Maine's economic future. He abandoned his Bangor law practice and turned his untiring energy to the development of Maine railroads. Poor generated the idea that Portland, with her magnificent harbor, should be linked by rail with Montreal and become Canada's winter sea outlet.

Poor personally surveyed the terrain for the best route and persuaded Portlanders to apply to the legislature for a charter and raise money to help finance the project. Spurred on by Poor, Portland merchants and businessmen took up the enterprise with enthusiasm. Edward H. Elwell, a business historian of the period, notes: "It was a revival movement — a revival of enterprise, a revival of business, a revival of prosperity, — and everybody but a few croakers was converted. The city loaned its credit bonds to the amount of $2,000,000."

Portland was not the only city making overtures to Montreal. Boston was also interested. Although Boston was half a day by ocean transport further away from Europe than Portland, and one hundred miles further from Montreal, she fully appreciated the benefits of being Montreal's winter port. Poor fought to prevent Montreal from choosing Boston. He made a heroic sleigh ride to Montreal in the teeth of a blinding northeast blizzard to thwart the Bostonians. After driving all night Poor arrived just as the Montreal Board of Trade was considering the Boston route and he successfully persuaded Montreal to postpone action.

Atlantic & St. Lawrence Railroad Locomotive

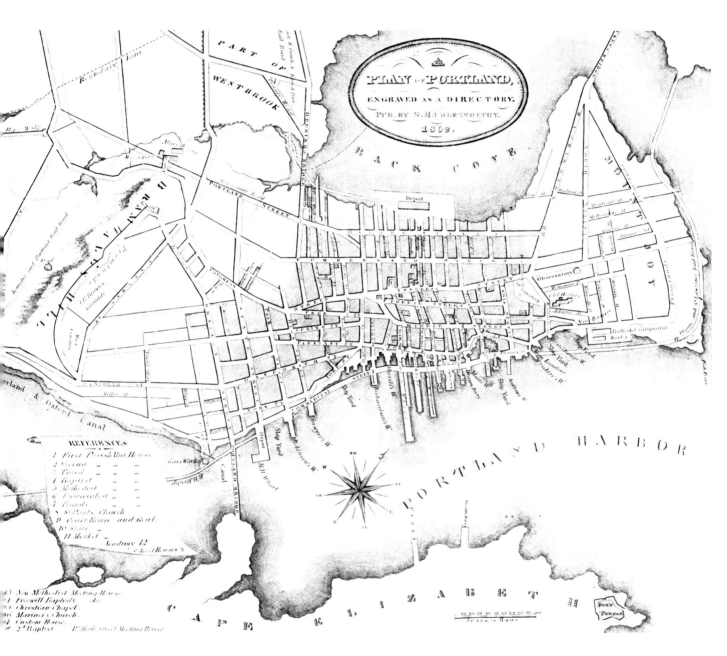

Competition between Boston and Portland grew bitter. Newspaper editors dreamed up the idea of a race between the two cities to determine which could deliver a letter faster from England to Montreal. In March, 1847, two steamers carrying the letters left England — one for Boston, the other for Portland. Portlanders watched eagerly from the Observatory as their ship docked. Horsemen were ready for the dash to Montreal. With the American flag flying and whips cracking, the sleigh carrying the Portland letter reached Montreal four hours ahead of its Boston rival. It had made the two hundred and fifty mile journey in eighteen hours and sixteen minutes! Portland won the route.

The Atlantic & St. Lawrence Railroad, later taken over by the Grand Trunk, brought carloads of grain to Portland from Canada and the west for reshipment. The prosperity it brought to Portland exceeded even John Poor's dreams.

The coming of the railroad spurred the city to undertake another enterprising scheme. To handle rail shipments more efficiently, the Atlantic & St. Lawrence urged the city to fill in the waterfront below Fore Street and build a new street. This could link the Portland, Saco & Portsmouth terminal at the foot of High Street with that of the Atlantic & St. Lawrence near the foot of India Street. The city agreed and by 1853 Commercial Street, over a mile long and a hundred feet wide, with twenty-six feet in the center for railroad tracks, was completed. The $80,000 expanse, lined with new warehouses and wharves, soon became the hub of Portland's booming import and export business.

John A. Poor

Concurrently, more land was being made on the back side of the peninsula. Cumberland Avenue had originally bordered Back Cove. By 1857 Kennebec and Lincoln Streets had been constructed over the flats and plans were being made to circle Munjoy Hill with a wide avenue which would eventually connect with Commercial Street.

51

THE ROOTS OF CULTURE

In New England, the decades preceding the Civil War witnessed a vast expansion of cultural activities. Van Wyck Brooks called this period in American history the flowering of New England. With more money in their pockets and more leisure as their business interests expanded, Portlanders turned their attention to a fuller enjoyment and encouragement of the arts.

Henry Wadsworth Longfellow was one of the literary giants of the age. As a Bowdoin undergraduate, he wrote his father, "I most eagerly aspire after future eminence in literature. My whole soul burns most ardently for it and every earthly thought centers upon it."

No poet of his day was more widely read; *Hiawatha* sold ten thousand copies in four weeks. *Evangeline, The Courtship of Miles Standish, the Midnight Ride of Paul Revere* delighted readers everywhere in the civilized world. Longfellow was the first American author to be honored by having his bust in the Poet's Corner at Westminster Abbey.

His Portland roots ran deep. One grandfather had been a Revolutionary War hero; the other helped found Bowdoin College; his father, Stephen, was an eminent Portland lawyer. The Longfellows built Portland's first brick house and owned the first piano in town. Many of Longfellow's poems were influenced by his early days in Portland. On March 29, 1855, he wrote in his journal, "At night as I lie in bed, a poem comes into my mind — a memory of Portland, my native town, the city by the sea." The next day he wrote *My Lost Youth*, which praised Portland as the beautiful town seated by the sea.

Longfellow made his home in Cambridge where he taught at Harvard, but he returned to Portland for frequent visits. His life had more than its share of grief. His first wife, Mary Storer Potter of Portland, died four years after their marriage while they were traveling in Europe; his second wife Frances Elizabeth Appleton burned to death in their Cambridge home. Longfellow's face was painfully burned when he tried to put out the flames and so

53

Longfellow, bronze by Franklin Simmons

scarred that he was unable to shave and wore a beard the rest of his life. Whenever his spirits were at a low ebb, a visit to Portland seemed to restore him. He spent many summers writing here. He visited Portland shortly before his death in 1882 and wrote in his journal, "Portland has lost none of its charm."

Three members of the Nathaniel Willis family also pursued writing careers. The father, Nathaniel, founded Portland's long-lived *Eastern Argus* in 1803. Known as a fighting editor after losing a libel suit in a bitter Congressional campaign, he continued to publish his newspaper from jail. His son, N. P. Willis, served as a foreign correspondent for the *New York Mirror*. His column, *Pencilings By the Way*, fed avid U.S. readers gossipy tidbits about Europe's important people. James Russell Lowell called N. P. Willis the "topmost bright bubble on the wave of the town." His sister, Sarah Willis Parton, wrote under the pen name of Fanny Fern. In 1853 her *Fern Leaves From Fanny's Portfolio* was a best seller with over 70,000 copies sold.

William Willis, Portland's most valuable historian, was only distantly related. In 1849 he edited and annotated the *Journals of the Reverend Thomas Smith and the Reverend Samuel Deane*, pastors of the First Church in Portland. His own *History of Portland, 1832-1864*, is a definitive resource to historians today.

In addition to Mrs. Parton, other women enhanced Portland literary circles. Madame Sally Wood, who wrote early in the nineteenth century as "A Lady from Maine," was one of America's first novelists to use local characters and scenes. Mrs. Elizabeth Akers, wife of the Portland sculptor, Paul Akers, according to author-critic John Neal, set half the editors of our country by their ears, with her poem published in the 1860's: *Rock Me to Sleep, Mother*, which was later made into a popular ballad.

Mrs. Elizabeth Oakes Smith not only wrote, but also lectured on women's rights. She was the attractive wife of Seba Smith who started the first daily newspaper in Maine, *The Portland Courier*, in 1829 and won fame as a humorist with his nationally read "Jack Downing Letters" lampooning downeast people. In a day when women were expected to sew a fine seam

View of Portland, 1850

and not express themselves on issues, Mrs. Smith charmed audiences with her wit and wisdom. She became one of the first women to join the lyceum movement.

The lyceum movement, with its public lectures on every conceivable subject, was part of a national effort to further popular education. Portland was caught up in the nationwide fervor of intellectual improvement. In 1803 Portland Academy for Boys opened its doors with fiery Edward Payson (who later became the pastor of the Second Parish Church) as headmaster.

55

John Neal

In 1831 Westbrook Seminary became one of the first institutions in the United States to offer coeducational facilities. Portland had the first tax-supported public high school in the state. A library had been started as early as 1799.

In 1815 The Maine Charitable Mechanic Association was founded to educate mechanics. It soon added a library and every winter sponsored a course of lectures upon subjects of the highest interest. Newspapers promoted political views as well as local literary efforts. Longfellow's poem "The Battle of Lovell's Pond" appeared in the *Portland Gazette* when he was only twelve years old. By 1860 eleven newspapers, mostly weeklies, were published locally.

Perhaps the most colorful and controversial of Portland's literary figures was John Neal. Not meeting success in law or trade, self-educated Neal turned to literature and became a prolific writer. In England, where Neal spent several years, he was considered the most original and arresting American writer of his day. He wrote an autobiography, *Wandering Recollections of a Somewhat Busy Life,* two definitive works about his beloved Portland, several novels (he turned out one three-volume novel in twenty-seven days!), an epic poem, literary criticism, and innumerable articles. His best writing was vigorous and dashing, his worst long-winded and disorganized. He said of his own novel *Logan* that it should be taken as people take opium, "A grain may exhilarate – more may stupefy – much will be death."

Neal's book, *Portland Illustrated,* published in 1874, gives us an intimate picture of the city. Portlanders did not always appreciate Neal's infatuation with his native city and sometimes called him "Crazy Neal." He was indeed eccentric, but also public spirited and generous. He was a champion of all kinds of causes from women's rights to the founding of Portland's first gymnasium. Portlanders were not unaware of Neal's influence on the development of art in their city. He was Portland's first art patron. The *Portland Transcript* of March 5, 1884 says, "He supplied the necessary elements of criticism and patronage, and

*"View from
Simonton's Cove,"
now Willard Beach,
by John B. Hudson, Jr.*

"Tow Path," by Charles F. Kimball

it is not too much to say his influence went far to encourage the cultivation of art among us."

"Scene on the Maine Coast," by Harrison B. Brown

Neal did much to help Portland's talented artists. The Maine Charitable Mechanic Association Fair in 1838 was the first opportunity for Portland painters to exhibit publicly. Charles Codman, Portland's first professional landscape artist, and Charles O. Cole, Portland's leading portrait painter, dominated the show. Cole made a good living painting Portland's prominent citizens. Longfellow sat for him and once while doing so wrote, "Sitting occupies several hours of the morning, and will send me down to posterity with a face as red as Lord Morpeth's fiery waistcoat." Perhaps Longfellow's patience gave out. The painting hangs unfinished in the Longfellow house.

59

Charles Codman was a sign painter and a clock decorator until John Neal discovered his work. Neal was charmed by the free handling, sprightliness and brave drawing of his trees. Codman had caught the lights in the foliage by going over the leafing with a pin. Neal found commissions for Codman and started him on his successful career as a landscape artist.

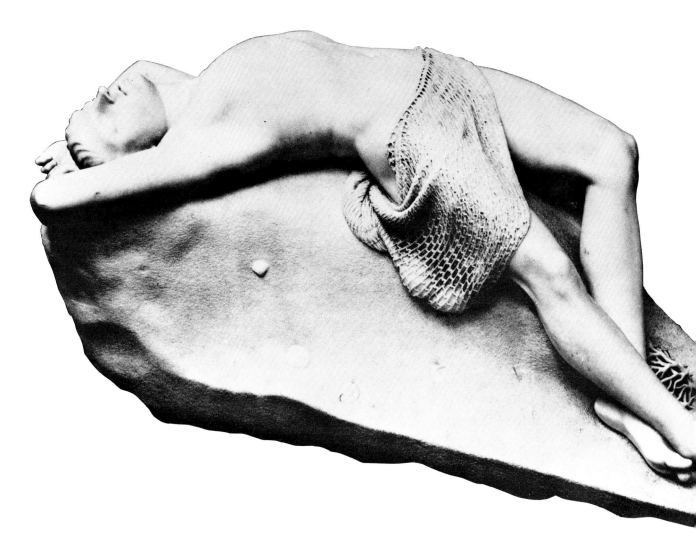

"Dead Pearl Diver," marble by Paul Akers

Neal helped Portland's sculptors Franklin Simmons and Paul Akers. Simmons progressed from a bust of Neal to statues of such notables as Ulysses S. Grant and Admiral David Farragut. Neal wrote that Akers had a strong sense of individuality and a capital memory for features. He set up a studio where Akers could work. Neal also encouraged Akers' friend John Rollin Tilton, (whom he discovered painting railroad car panels for thirty cents a panel) to become a landscape painter. Akers and Tilton both left Portland for Italy, where Akers produced his "Dead Pearl Diver," now in the permanent collection of the Portland Society of Art. Tilton painted landscapes and scenes for tourists, some of which he exhibited at London's Royal Academy.

Harrison B. Brown, probably Portland's most successful nineteenth century artist, also benefited from John Neal's advice and criticism. Brown, a sign painter, was attempting portraits as well as landscapes and marine scenes. Neal found his landscapes exuberant and overflowing with sunshine. Neal told him to forget the portraits and concentrate on landscapes. Brown followed the advice. His marine scenes with their dashing waves and rugged cliffs today are regarded by some collectors as minor masterpieces.

Charles F. Kimball and John B. Hudson, Jr. also painted here in the 1850's. Kimball, (married to the daughter of John Greenleaf Cloudman, a Portland portrait painter) was a stair builder and never considered himself a professional artist, insisting he did not wish to commercialize his work. Kimball excelled at summer landscapes such as his *Midsummer Day at Diamond Island*. He went on many sketching trips with his friend, Hudson, a competent watercolor artist of natural subjects.

PROHIBITION

While Portland's artists and authors were making noteworthy contributions to the flowering of New England, other Portlanders were caught up in various reform movements sweeping the country. From 1820 to 1860 deep concern for such social causes as women's rights, peace, temperance, treatment of criminals and the insane, and the abolition of slavery pervaded America. Neal Dow, a Portland contemporary of Longfellow, acquired national fame as the leader of the temperance movement.

Portlanders had been heavy drinkers since Revolutionary times when Alice Greele's tavern had been a favorite meeting place for baked beans and mugs of flip. Burgoyne's surrender is said to have been celebrated excessively with drinks passed out the tavern window and cannons fired so exuberantly that one celebrant was shot to death.

Drinking was not confined to taverns. Every grocery store had its department for drinking with its casks of rum and gin and tubs of punch to attract customers. The profitable West Indies trade made liquor readily available. It flowed at every social and public gathering – town meetings, military musters, Fourth of July celebrations, weddings and even funerals. The most important moments in the workingman's day were his rum breaks. At eleven and again at four o'clock a bell was rung, masons came down from their ladders, joiners dropped their tools, and workers stopped "to take some support."

Neal Dow in his *Reminiscences* says there were always fights in those days. Drunkenness was universal. Workingmen's dwellings were shabby and their children poorly fed and clothed as wages were freely spent on demon rum. Maine's two leading industries, lumbering and fishing, separated men from their families for long stretches of time and they sought solace in liquor. Dow judged that Maine people probably consumed more intoxicating liquor in proportion to their numbers than the people of any other state.

A Quaker, Neal Dow devoted his life to abolishing drunkenness and the evils accompanying it. Dow was a descendant of Hate Evil Hall and he more than lived up to his ancestor's name. After much political maneuvering, the Maine legislature passed in 1851 "An Act for the Suppression of Drinking

Neal Dow

Houses and Tippling Shops," which forbade the manufacture
and sale of liquor. The Maine Law was the first prohibition
law to be passed in the United States. It became a national
model and was copied by many other states before national
prohibition was enacted in 1920. Dow traveled and wrote, ex-
plaining his law and promoting the crusade against alcohol.
He ran for the presidency on the Prohibition ticket in 1880.

64

Although Dow won world-wide recognition as the "prophet of prohibition," his zeal and determination did not always endear him to his fellow Portlanders. As mayor of Portland he personally saw to it that his beloved act was rigidly enforced. He poured more than one dealer's liquor down the sewer and had all shipments coming into Portland searched, much to the annoyance of local merchants. While he was mayor, a man was shot to death when a mob tried to get the city's supply of medicinal liquor from the basement of Military Hall. Many Portlanders were enraged (including his cousin John Neal) when they found themselves the subjects of a short story, *History of a Neighborhood,* published in a New York temperance magazine. It was about intemperance on a fine street, which many recognized as Portland's aristocratic State Street.

Nothing deterred Dow. He was single-minded and completely devoted to his cause. He wrote, "I have not allowed myself to be concerned as to what others may have thought of me. He who swerves from what he believes to be his duty, through fear of ridicule or opposition of his neighbors, can accomplish little or nothing." Although he did not live to see it, Dow's goal was achieved with national prohibition, a testament to his considerable impact on American life.

CIVIL WAR

Of all the reform movements sweeping mid-nineteenth century America, none roused men's passions or stirred as much controversy as the movement to abolish slavery. It was the burning issue of the age, and Portland did not escape its flames.

Portland's Reverend Elijah Kellogg, who wrote boys' books about the Maine coast in addition to preaching, pointed out that conscience, self-interest and the law of God were pitted against each other on the slavery question. Portlanders were far from unanimous in their response to it. Many (such as George

65

*"Blowing up of cutter Caleb Cushing,
June 27, 1863" by Harrison B. Brown*

Evans and John Neal) agreed with the approach of the American Colonization Society which aimed at raising money to buy slaves and help them by sending them back to Africa. Others were inspired by William Lloyd Garrison's abolitionist movement which believed that slavery was a moral sin and that "immediate emancipation is the duty of the master and the right of the slave." Samuel Fessenden, a respected and prominent Portland lawyer, was greatly influenced by Garrison when he spoke in Portland and became a leader of the Maine Anti-Slavery Society.

Feelings ran high on both sides. When Stephen Foster appeared at Military Hall he was mobbed by the anti-abolitionists. Anti-slavery people were considered fanatics. The churches, with the exception of the Quakers, were not strong abolitionists. Some ministers defended slavery from the Bible; and the *Christian Mirror,* published in Portland, was hostile to the abolitionist cause. When the mayor refused to let the Maine Anti-Slavery Society hold a convention in City Hall, the Quakers offered their church and a mob tried to break up the meeting.

Portland had close economic ties with the South which made many less than enthusiastic for the movement to dethrone King Cotton and abolish slavery. John Bryce Carroll, Charles Clapp's son-in-law, who built the Carroll Mansion, was a Southerner dealing in tobacco; and Ruggles Sylvester Morse, who built the Victoria Mansion was a Southern sympathizer with interests in New Orleans. Other Portland merchants and shippers also had close and profitable commercial ties with the South. Abolitionist Austin Willey in his book *Slavery in Maine and the Nation,* claimed, "The whole coast was held in nearly absolute bondage."

By the 1850's the abolitionist movement had gathered momentum. The Liberty and the Free Soil political parties as well as anti-slavery Democrats were active in Maine. Harriet Beecher Stowe's *Uncle Tom's Cabin* and the passage of the Fugitive Slave Law aroused indignation in Portland as well as the rest of the North, and Portland became an active way station on the unlawful underground railroad.

When Fort Sumter was fired on and Lincoln called for 75,000 volunteers, Maine responded by supplying the Union's Army and Navy with more men proportionately than any other state. One quarter of the troops at the first disastrous Battle of Bull Run were men from Maine. Maine seamen and ships helped make the Union blockade of the South successful. Portland sent 5,000 men to war; four hundred and twenty-one surrendered their lives.

Although far from the armed conflict, one dramatic incident brought the excitement of war to Portland's doorstep. On the night of June 26, 1863, a daring Rebel navy officer, Lieutenant Charles W. Read, with twenty Confederate seamen aboard a captured fishing schooner, stole into Portland Harbor under the shadows of Fort Preble and Fort Gorges. (Ironically, Fort Gorges was begun two years before the Civil War by the Confederacy's President, Jefferson Davis, when he was United States Secretary of War.) They seized the U.S. revenue cutter *Caleb Cushing* and headed for the open sea. When the loss was discovered, Portland's mayor, Captain Jacob McLellan, and the Collector of Customs, Jedediah Jewett swiftly organized two parties of armed men aboard the steamer *Chesapeake* and the packet *Forest City* and pursued the Rebel force. The wind died down. The Confederates aboard the fleeing sailing ship became helplessly becalmed. As the *Chesapeake* drew nearer, Read set fire to his prize. It blew up with a tremendous explosion. The Confederates took to their boats but were captured and brought back to Portland as prisoners of war.

THE GREAT FIRE

On July 4, 1866, as the city was preparing to celebrate Independence Day and the end of the Civil War, disaster again struck and Portland suffered the greatest fire calamity the country had seen up to that time. Parades, fireworks and a balloon ascension had been planned to enliven the festivities. Tragically, the holiday which had begun so happily, ended in a night of terror and destruction.

A flicked cigar ash or perhaps a tossed firecracker started a small fire in a boat yard on Commercial Street. From the boat

yard the blaze spread to a nearby lumber yard and then to Brown's Sugarhouse on Maple Street (which was considered impregnable). It jumped the brick walls surrounding the building and melted the steel shutters on the windows and the roof of galvanized iron and tar. The building became a roaring inferno. A strong south wind whipped the flames to uncontrollable fury. Water was pumped from the city's reservoirs, wells, and even the harbor. It was a useless effort. Firefighters were powerless in the face of the conflagration which raged all night,

"Looking down Congress Street,"
by George F. Morse

The great fire at Portland (shaded area), July 4th, 1866

sweeping diagonally across the heart of the city from Commercial Street to Back Cove and to Munjoy Hill where it finally burned itself out.

Remarkably, in that disastrous holocaust, only two reported deaths were verified. The net property loss was calculated at six million dollars, more than a quarter of the city's assessed valuation. The loss in historic landmarks, private and public, is of course incalculable. The customs house, post office, city hall, churches, hotels, newspaper offices, lawyers' offices, book shops and retail stores, and the city's wholesale and dry goods

72

houses lining Middle Street were gone. Eighteen hundred buildings in all were destroyed; nearly ten thousand Portlanders were homeless. The fire gutted old family mansions as indiscriminately as it did the tenements of the poor. Many of the city's gracious elms were consumed in the flames; neighborhoods were reduced to charred ruins with an occasional blackened chimney left standing.

Longfellow, visiting Portland a month later, wrote, "I have been in Portland since the fire. Desolation! Desolation! Desolation! It reminds me of Pompeii, the 'sepult city'."

ELMS, LOCUST STREET.

73

1866-1912

FROM THE ASHES

HARPER'S WEEKLY.

A JOURNAL OF CIVILIZATION.

VOL. X.—No. 500.]   NEW YORK, SATURDAY, JULY 28, 1866.   [SINGLE COPIES TEN CENTS. $4.00 PER YEAR IN ADVANCE.

Entered according to Act of Congress, in the Year 1866, by Harper & Brothers, in the Clerk's Office of the District Court for the Southern District of New York.

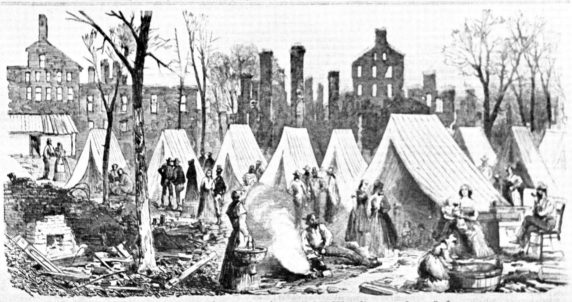

GREAT FIRE IN PORTLAND, MAINE—TENTS AMONG THE RUINS.—[SKETCHED BY STANLEY FOX.]

THE PORTLAND FIRE.

No fire which has ever been inflicted upon an American town has been so ruinous, in its propor- tion of loss to the wealth of the city, as that which, beginning in Portland on the evening of July 4, raged with unabated fury for over twenty-four hours, destroying before its close one-third of the city. When the morning papers of this great sea- port announced on the morning of the 4th that the pyrotechnic display of that evening would be of un- usual magnificence, they did not foresee in what direful sense their prediction would be fulfilled be- fore the day closed.

The fire began, it seems, in a small boat-builder's shop between Commercial and Fore Streets. It

GREAT FIRE IN PORTLAND, MAINE—DISTRIBUTING FOOD TO THE CITIZENS AT THE OLD CITY HALL.—[SKETCHED BY STANLEY FOX.]

POST-WAR RECOVERY

The ashes were still smoldering when Portlanders turned to the hard task of rebuilding. Their town had been destroyed by Indians; it had been bombarded by the British; but they did not know the word despair. They went to work.

Led by Mayor Augustus E. Stevens and his relief committee, everyone pitched in to help. A city of tents for the homeless sprang up on Munjoy Hill. Soup kitchens ladled out food to the needy; relief supplies poured into Portland from all over the United States. The debris was cleared away and rebuilding commenced immediately. Fortunately, the favorable weather during the summer of 1866 made tent living easier and helped speed the rebuilding. So great was the public effort and enthusiasm that Portland seemed to rise from its ashes like the legendary phoenix, a more modern and impressive city than she had been before the holocaust.

The business and financial sections on Middle and Exchange Streets had been particularly hard-hit by the fire. They were almost completely rebuilt with stylish brick Victorian structures. Before the fire Middle Street had been half residential. Now it was transformed into a business thoroughfare and, together with rebuilt Exchange Street, gained eminence as the financial and commercial heart of the city, a reputation it enjoys to this day.

Businessmen showed their confidence in Portland's future by investing vast sums to rebuild. John Neal claimed that "a new spirit took sudden possession of our property-holders . . . and straightway they began building for the future, so Portland is now . . . at least fifty years ahead of what she would have been otherwise."

Some businesses, like Byron Greenough and Company, were able to collect their insurance and immediately start reconstruction. Others were not so fortunate. The losses were so great that many local insurance companies could not meet their payments. This added hardship did not deter Portland businessmen. Handsome new stores were built by Deering and Milliken Company, Bailey and Noyes, and many other firms. J. B. Brown built the elegant Falmouth Hotel on Middle Street. William Widgery Thomas, president of the Canal Bank, had his bank rebuilt with a symbolic phoenix carved over the door. Block after block of modern brick buildings went up, transforming the scarred city into a modern metropolis.

Maine General Hospital, Francis H. Fassett architect, dedicated 1874

Public construction kept pace with private initiative. A new city hall rose on the present site, and a new marble post office was built on Middle and Exchange Streets. A $485,000 granite customs house, a far cry from the pine shed which had originally housed the Portland Collector of Customs, was built on Commercial Street. In 1868 plans were drafted for the Maine General Hospital to be built on the site of the state arsenal on Bramhall Hill. Portlanders raised $100,000 toward its construction through fairs, sales and donations. The modern hospital facility with its lovely view of the White Mountains was accepting patients by 1874.

An able and foresighted mayor, Stevens saw to it that good planning accompanied the rebuilding. Pearl Street, for example, was extended across the city from the harbor to Back Cove. Other streets were widened and straightened. The fire had pointed up the need for an adequate city water supply and in 1868 Mayor Stevens signed a contract to pipe Sebago Lake water to Portland. The city authorities created Lincoln Park, Portland's first public recreational area, by buying up the land bounded by Pearl, Congress and Franklin Streets for $86,703. They did not want tenements rebuilt there and hoped the open space would serve as a firebreak. Inspired by the recovery made from the fire, the new park was originally called Phoenix Square.

It was truly a remarkable recovery. Within two years the city was almost completely rebuilt and a new era of prosperity and growth had been initiated.

The railroads were the basis for much of the city's economic vitality. Thanks to the railroads, Portland became a transportation center and a major exporting port. By 1872, sixty-five trains a day were stopping in Portland. The city had direct connections to New York with the Portland-Rochester line and to Boston with the Eastern Railroad and the Boston and Maine. The branches of the Maine Central connected Portland with upstate Maine, making it the main artery for moving goods into that expanding region. The Grand Trunk not only had direct lines to New Hampshire, Vermont and Montreal, but

Steamship "Great Eastern"

also provided rail connections with the expanding West.

Most western commerce was shipped via the Great Lakes to Montreal and then down the St. Lawrence. In winter, however, when the St. Lawrence froze, goods had to be shipped by rail to a more southern port for reloading on transatlantic cargo ships. The Grand Trunk made Portland Montreal's winter port. Large amounts of western as well as Canadian grain were brought to Portland for reshipment. In 1875, the Grand Trunk built the first of three huge grain elevators on the Portland waterfront. It held over 200,000 bushels of grain. Almost 22 million bushels of grain were received here during the winter of 1899, Portland's peak year. Fifty-eight per cent of this was shipped out as foreign export.

The Grand Trunk also gave impetus to steamship travel. The Canadian government subsidized a weekly steamship service to Liverpool, using Portland as its terminus during the winter months. Except for the sturdy down-easters in the 1870's and 1880's and the great five- and six-masted vessels still operating into the twentieth century, (carrying coal and Maine granite in the coastal trade and venturing as far as South America for Chilean nitrate and Peruvian copper and guano), the age of sail was ending. Steamboats were the wave of the future.

Portlanders were early transatlantic steamship enthusiasts. Back in the 1850's they had subscribed over $60,000 to build two huge piers at the foot of Munjoy Hill large enough to accommodate the gigantic English steamship *Great Eastern*. The huge 692-foot leviathan with its 112 furnaces was so big, it had to be launched sideways. On the trial run explosions occurred and years later the skeleton of a dead riveter was found trapped in the hull. The ill-fated steam monster was a financial failure and never made its anticipated docking in Portland.

The *Great Eastern* wharves, however, had their moment of glory in 1860 when Queen Victoria's son, the Prince of Wales, visited Portland. Unfortunately the royal departure was marred when an enthusiastic lady, unable to present her welcoming bouquet because of the crowds, threw it and knocked

Embarkation of the Prince of Wales from the Great Eastern Dock, Portland, October 20, 1860

the Prince's hat into Portland harbor. This unhappy experience did not dim Portland's enthusiasm for steamboats; steamship travel on a less grandiose scale later became an important means of transportation. There were tri-weekly runs from Portland to Bangor and New York and daily trips to Boston.

Steamboat travel was usually safe and reliable, but one disaster still serves as a grim warning to local seamen. The wooden side-wheeler *Portland* left Boston on November 26, 1898, with between 140 and 190 people aboard. Although the captain had received warnings of snow and strong recommendations not to sail, he decided to head for Portland on schedule. She was

82

never seen again. It was one of the worst blizzards of the century. Many Portland families were affected by this sea tragedy.

Steamship travel, immigration and the operations of the Grand Trunk all helped to make the port of Portland boom during the late nineteenth and early twentieth centuries. Seven or more transatlantic steamer lines operated out of Portland. As a port of entry, too, the city prospered. During the 1890's over 4,000 foreign immigrants a year entered America by way of Portland harbor. Millions of tons of wheat, livestock and cargo were shipped by means of the Grand Trunk operations to Europe each winter. The total value of imports and exports in 1872 was $45,000,000.

Fish continued to be an important export. By 1860 the value of Maine fisheries exceeded a million dollars a year. Portland fisherman competed with Marblehead in their cod catch. Lumber was another big export with as many as thirty lumber concerns doing business on Commercial Street. In August, 1874, nearly six million feet were shipped to the west Indies. After the peak year of 1868, however, molasses imports from the West Indies fell off, although lumber continued to be shipped there. Molasses had become an unprofitable item after Maine prohibition laws closed the distilleries. A new system of sugar refining was developed which enabled shipments to be made in bags rather than boxes and in bulk rather than hogsheads. Many other commodities were imported. The Collector of Customs' income during the 1880's averaged $900,000 a year.

Portland's prosperity was based not only on her railway connections, her harbor and the happy circumstances which made her Canada's winter sea outlet, but also on her industrial growth. A variety of industries developed. Portland produced everything from paints and brushes to artificial legs. From 1864 to 1873 The Portland Glass Factory produced superior quality glass. Mrs. Lincoln is reputed to have bought a set for the White House. If true, it is a monument to her good taste, as today the lovely pieces are considered collectors' items. Schotterbeck and Company made Portland Obstetric Forceps which doctors and mothers appreciated as they were "never known to slip." The Star Match Company exported matches to many foreign countries, and the Portland Stoneware Company made excellent drainpipes which were sold nationwide.

The city's world-wide reputation as a canning center began with the founding of the Portland Packing Company. The firm, started in 1863 by James P. Baxter and William G. Davis, originated a method of packing green corn in tins. It earned an excellent reputation as the food's natural flavor was preserved in the tins. Accurate weights and content descriptions appeared on the labels which were artistically designed and printed in London. The idea of a food's natural flavor being so preserved was an immediate success. When served, it was both fresh-looking and delicious. Sales soared. The Portland Packing Company became the largest food packing firm in the world with sales of more than three-quarters of a million dollars.

The profits from the Portland Packing Company made James P. Baxter a rich man at a young age. Fortunately for the welfare of the city, Baxter was able and willing to devote much of his life to varied cultural interests and the betterment of Portland. He served as president of the Maine Historical Society for thirty years. He was a competent historian himself and is responsible for much research and writing on Maine's early history. He founded and was the first president of the Portland Society of Art. He is responsible for starting the Portland Associated Charities, from which the United Fund developed. In 1888 he gave Portland its present public library and served as its president. His generosity, interests, and influence on Portland's cultural development, were deep and lasting.

Perhaps Baxter's most praiseworthy contribution to Portland was the part he played in creating the city's park system. Modern Portland has over four hundred acres of public parks. Much of this recreational area was acquired while Baxter was mayor of the city. When in 1893 he was first elected, he dreamed of ringing the city with green tree-shaded areas; during his six terms in office he worked tirelessly to make his dream a reality.

When the Eastern and Western Promenades had been laid out in 1836, they had been on the edge of town. Much of the land surrounding them had remained in private hands, increasing in value as the areas became prime residential real estate. As mayor, Baxter convinced the city to buy up the privately owned land on the water side of the Eastern Promenade and arranged the exchange with the J. B. Brown heirs of a piece of city-owned land for their land on the northwestern slopes of the Western Promenade. Baxter also encouraged the city to add more land to Deering's Oaks, which had been given to the city by Nathaniel and Henry Deering in 1879.

Portland Glass, c. 1865

85

James Phinney Baxter

The project closest to Baxter's heart was the building of a boulevard along Back Cove. Baxter hired the landscape architects, Olmsted Brothers of Boston, to plan the course of the road and at his own expense took the city council to Boston to study its promenades and parks. He negotiated with the landowners around the Cove and convinced them to relinquish a one hundred-foot strip of land, reassuring them that the proposed boulevard would improve the value of their properties. By 1905 construction was underway, and the boulevard was eventually named after James P. Baxter, the man whose vision and effort had made it possible.

POLITICAL LEADERSHIP

During the last half of the nineteenth century, Portland politicians made outstanding contributions, not only to their city, but to their state and nation. Maine justified its reputation for sending men of character and ability to Congress; whether they were Whig, Democrat or Republican, they served with distinction. Many, if not elected from Portland, made Portland their home at some time during their lives.

Both Hannibal Hamlin and James G. Blaine served with Portland newspapers in their early careers. Blaine was on the editorial staff of the *Portland Advertiser* for a short time. He wrote his mother that Portland was a very beautiful but expensive city. He preferred Augusta, where he bought an interest in the *Kennebec Journal.* He was an orator with magnetic charm and a remarkable memory for names and earned the title of the "plumed knight of American politics." He served in the House and Senate and became the Republican nominee for President in 1884, losing to Grover Cleveland. As Secretary of State he served his country with distinction, improving relations with South America and creating the Pan-American Union.

*Portland Public Library,
gift of James P. Baxter, 1888*

87

Hannibal Hamlin studied law in Samuel Fessenden's Portland law firm and published *The Jeffersonian.* While still a young man, he moved to Hampden and launched his political career. He was firmly opposed to slavery. When the Democrats drew up a platform favoring slavery in 1856, he announced to the Senate that he was leaving the Democratic party forever. He became a Republican and was elected Lincoln's vice-president.

Judge Nathan Clifford remained a loyal Democrat throughout his life. This was not an easy decision in a politically chaotic age when the slavery issue forced many men to shift their party loyalties. Blaine once called the Portland native "an ingrained hungry Democrat, double-dyed and dyed-in-the-wool, and coarse wool at that." Clifford served two terms in the House of Representatives, was U.S. Attorney General and Minister to Mexico. In 1858 Buchanan appointed him to the "New England" seat on the United States Supreme Court. He served ably until incapacitated by an apoplectic stroke in 1880, but refused to resign from the Supreme Court bench until a Democratic President could appoint his successor. At the time of his death, the Republican *New York Tribune,* in spite of its earlier opposition, called him "a jurist of learning and integrity."

Ex-Congressman George Evans made Portland his home. He was a Whig and had served in both the House and the Senate. John Quincy Adams called him "one of the ablest men and most eloquent orators in Congress." Although a man of first-rate ability, conservative Evans underestimated the political impact of the slavery issue and would not become a Republican when the Whig party died out. His political career ended there and he devoted his energies to a growing Portland law practice.

When Governor Israel Washburn retired from the political arena, he, too, moved to Portland, where he spent his last twenty years. Israel was the eldest of seven remarkable brothers born in Maine, who scattered across the United States to become successful bankers, industrialists, editors and politicians. He served in the U.S. Congress at the same time as two of his brothers; Elihu, representing Illinois, and Cadwallader, Wis-

Governor Israel Washburn

88

consin. Gaillard Hunt describes Israel Washburn as "a solid, hard-working man of sound knowledge and rigid integrity." Opposed to the extension of slavery, he was one of the founders of the Republican party and is credited by some with suggesting the title Republican as the new party's name. He was a strong Civil War governor. When Maine was asked for two regiments to fight for the Union, Washburn called a special session of the legislature and sent ten. Abraham Lincoln showed Israel Washburn his appreciation by appointing him the Portland Collector of Customs.

Two political giants who represented Portland in Congress for many years were William Pitt Fessenden and Thomas Brackett Reed. Both were exceptional men.

Hon. William Pitt Fessenden

Fessenden served as a congressman and senator from 1854 to 1869, and as Lincoln's Secretary of the Treasury. The son of abolitionist Samuel Fessenden, he entered the Senate in 1854 when the Kansas-Nebraska Act was being debated. This act voided the Missouri Compromise and allowed the extension of slavery. The speech he made opposing passage of the act caused a Southerner to comment, "Why, what a man is this! All his guns are double-shotted." Fessenden was a man of rigid integrity. As a congressman he voted against $6,000 pork-barrel legislation benefiting Portland harbor, saying he would vote against all such measures benefiting privileged sections of the country and was willing to begin with his own.

After the Civil War Fessenden wielded great power as the chairman of the Joint Congressional Committee on Reconstruction, which planned the restoration of the Southern states to the Union. His finest hour was the Johnson impeachment trial. He was one of only seven Republicans who did not buckle under the extraordinary pressures of the radicals dominating his party. As John F. Kennedy points out in his *Profiles in Courage,* Fessenden thought, "the whole thing is a mere madness . . . whatever may be the consequences to myself personally, whatever I may think and feel as a politician, I will not decide the question against my own judgment . . . I shall at all events

retain my own self-respect and a clear conscience, and time will do justice to my motives at least."

Portland sent Thomas Brackett Reed to Congress from 1876 to 1899. He served as Speaker of the House three times. He was noted for his large physique (6' 3", 275 pounds), his wit and his brilliant parliamentary ability. He was mentioned for the Republican nomination for President in 1892 and 1896. When asked about his chances for receiving the nomination, he answered, "They could do worse, and they probably will." During his first term as Speaker of the House, Reed earned the nickname, "Czar." He forced Congress to adopt "Reed's Rules" of procedure which made the silent quorum impossible. This tactic had been used to paralyze legislation. Congressmen not answering the roll were not counted toward a quorum, even though they were present in their seats. When Reed counted the silent Democrats present, pandemonium resulted. Reed stood firm, requesting those "members who say they are not present to please be seated."

Reed could be most sarcastic. His definition of a statesman was "a successful politician who is dead." He once said of two opponents, "They never open their mouths without subtracting from the sum of human knowledge." When a congressman said he'd rather be right than be President, Reed assured him, "Don't worry, you'll never be either."

Reed heartily opposed the Spanish American War and the annexation of Hawaii and the Philippines. Deciding to end his brilliant Congressional career and resign, he wrote his Maine constituents, "Whatever may happen, I am sure the First Maine District will always be true to the principles of liberty, self-government and the rights of man." Portland erected a statue in his honor on the Western Promenade.

THE PORTLAND SPIRIT

Mark Twain called the last years of the nineteenth century The Gilded Age. It was an era of opulent wealth and newly earned leisure. It brought the summer vacationer to Maine. The trek of city dwellers to the mountains and the sea became an annual phenomenon. It was the heyday of the summer resort and the beginning of Maine's booming tourist business.

A land and sea transportation center, Portland was the strategic point of entry. Wealthy families headed to Bar Harbor or Poland Spring for the season; less affluent artists and writers headed for a summer of painting or writing on Monhegan Island or Deer Isle. Many summer visitors didn't bother to travel beyond Portland for their vacations. They built or rented summer homes and cottages in Falmouth or out at Cape Elizabeth and Pine Point, and on the Casco Bay Islands.

The area also had its share of hotels, beaches, resorts and cool breezes. There were trolley parks less than an hour's ride away, and it was just a pleasant day's train excursion to the rolling surf at Old Orchard Beach, the fishing on Lake Sebago, or the delicious cuisine at the Crawford Notch House in the White Mountains.

The islands off Portland in Casco Bay were readily accessible by steamboats making frequent runs on regular schedules.

92

Weathly Canadians came to take in the view of Portland harbor from the rocking chairs on the piazzas of the Ottawa House on Cushing's Island, or to enjoy fish chowders at the Union House on Peak's Island. Some summer folk stayed for weeks of unhurried enjoyment picking blueberries, playing croquet, and rocking in the sea breezes. Campers and picnickers came for shorter periods. In the 1890's a day's outing might include a three-mile steamer trip to Peak's Island, a band concert or play by the island's repertory theater group, bowling and swinging at Greenwood amusement park, and hopefully a clambake, topped off by a moonlight boat ride back to Portland. Summer was a jolly, lazy time and the islands of Casco Bay held pleasures for all.

The wealth and leisure of the gilded age promoted cultural pursuits as well as vacations and pleasure seeking.

Perhaps Portland did not attract as many artists as Prout's Neck or Monhegan Island, but many talented ones painted here from time to time. Happily for Portland, art was sponsored and appreciated by those with the means to promote it. Margaret Mussey Sweat, a wealthy Portland author, wrote book reviews, travel books and *Ethel's Love Life,* the first Sapphic novel to be published in America. She willed the McLellan-Sweat Mansion to the Portland Society of Art and provided funds for an art museum.

The theater had a harder time getting off the ground in Portland. In the early days traveling troupes came to Portland occasionally, but a puritanical law had discouraged the building of a theater. Sometimes the law was circumvented and plays were presented between sections of a concert. But play production was not consistently profitable and producers were few. Maybe the fact that Portlanders had no theatrical entertainment to keep them up nights caused Anthony Trollope to comment in 1861, "O Happy Portlanders! If they only knew their good fortune. They get up early and go to bed early." As the nineteenth century wore on, various theaters were built and stock companies performed from time to time. John Wilkes Booth appeared in *Hamlet* before starring as the villain in the death of President Lincoln. The heyday of Portland theater came with the building of the Jefferson Theater in 1897. Then Portland audiences were rewarded with performances by such artists as Sarah Bernhardt in *Camille* and Maude Adams in *Peter Pan.*

Portland's exposure to good theater was intermittent, but music was always appreciated. From earliest times Maine people loved games, fun and music. Sewing bees, sleigh rides, church picnics and most social get-togethers were enlivened with song. Musical enjoyment was on a fairly informal basis until the advent of Hermann Kotzschmar.

A teacher and composer, Kotzschmar became Portland's undisputed musical leader. He served as organist of the First Parish Church for forty-seven years and as leader of the Haydn Association Chorus. Throughout his lifetime Kotzschmar favorably influenced the classical musical life of the city. When Portland's third city hall was built in 1912, Cyrus H. K. Curtis donated a $60,000 organ, the second largest in the world, in honor of his friend, Hermann Kotzschmar.

The new city hall was built on Congress Street. The old one in Market Square had been torn down to make way for Franklin Simmon's massive bronze statue. Entitled Our Lady of Victories, it belatedly honored the Civil War dead and Market

Square became known as Monument Square.

Throughout these years the character of Congress Street was changing. Commercial establishments, banks and fashionable shops and department stores lined its sidewalks. It was no longer the sole artery for cross-town traffic, but had become the center of the city's downtown business activity. People from the growing suburbs thronged to Congress Street to do their shopping and it is now Portland's busiest and most prosperous thoroughfare.

The new city hall, built of Maine granite, contains an auditorium seating three thousand, providing ample space for large audiences to enjoy a variety of social and cultural events. This unusual union of civic and cultural interests is symbolic of the spirit with which Portland began, and with which it greeted the twentieth century. It is a communal spirit of justified pride in her past and confidence in her future.

ARCHITECTURE

1785-1820

LATE COLONIAL AND FEDERAL STYLES

VIEW OF PORTLAND, ME

DRAWN FROM NATURE BY E. WHITEFIELD.

FROM THE CAPE ELIZABETH SIDE.

TOPOGRAPHY AND TEXTURES

Portland is a peninsula blessed with a topography that has favorably influenced its architectural development. A longitudinal, saddle-shaped land mass, it culminates in easterly and westerly promontories. The winding early streets — Fore, Middle and Back (now Congress Street)   retain their original pathlike nature; so do Danforth and Spring Streets. The shorter cross-peninsula accesses, Exchange, High, State and Park, while laid out with a more mathematical eye, happily profit from the hilly vagaries of the land. Even later streets like Bowdoin and Thomas, Spruce and Pine, preserve the informality of the older peninsula streets.

Unrestricted by the regularity imposed on architecture in an inflexible grid street pattern, the character of Portland's buildings and streetscapes is highly individual. In place of the uniform block-and-row development discernible in other cities of equal age, Portland's peninsula offers a delightful variety of architectural alternatives.

It is almost impossible to predict what view may be revealed at a turning; whether buildings will be tight to the street and their neighbors, or set off in urban isolation; whether an alley way or court may extend the neighborhood inward, or a sudden widening at an irregular intersection create a modest square. It is, in short, tempting to equate the idiosyncratic nature of the urban environment with traditional Maine individualism.

A unity, however, prevails in the richness of buildings and paving materials. Warm, red brick is everywhere in eighteenth, nineteenth and twentieth century buildings; in Federal mansions; in Victorian business blocks and picturesque dwellings. The theme is elaborated in fancy brickwork decoration well above eye-level and in the variety of paving patterns the pedestrian notes beneath his feet.

Appropriately, granite provides a counterpoint: in solid curbings and street pavings; in lintels set in brick façades; in stern grey store fronts and the occasional imposing public buildings made entirely of stone.

To the textural richness of brick and granite must be added the abundant and imaginative use of wood: linear clapboard structures enlivened by carved ornament; delicate porticos and balustrades completing brick buildings. Cast iron, brownstone, grey and rosy slate, marble and tile enhance the list of visual enjoyments.

Finally, nature has gradually furnished magnificent coherence in trees and other plantings. Enormous maples, varieties of evergreens and the famed Portland oaks, provide shade, protection and the visual gratification so important to one's aesthetic fulfillment. Elm trees, once the pride of our city, are rapidly disappearing, victims of the Dutch elm disease.

101

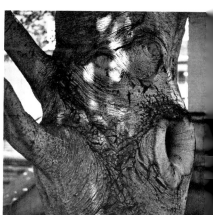

I think the sun might be placed higher above the horizon, or else left out entirely.
The street as you enter the Town is more than twice as wide as it should bee.
I suppose there should be another boat attempting to land at Mrs Cotton's
& armed men opposing it.
The Hay-market should be placed where the street divides.
The wharves should be nearer parallell with the cross streets than they are.
The roof of Doctor Watts's house should be shaped after this manner,

The roof of col Peebles thus, ; the roof of my house thus, ;

The roof of your shop thus, ; the roof of mr marstons house thus

the roofs of mr Codmans and Capt Boyntons thus

mr Codmans store from the Harbour appears thus, ... The rest m
be represented as having common, or pitch'd roofs:
One general fault that I observe is, that the low houses are made too sma
in proportion to the large ones.

mr Codmans lane should have been right against the front door of the me
house; and a little to the north East of it the lane that goes down between (
roses and Deacon Titcombs.

my house is 70 feet fr the west est part of the meeting house, the barn and
of the wood-house should appear between them.

The hill at the north east end of the neck is not near high enough. . . .

EARLY GROWTH OF STREET PATTERNS

Not all of the existing structures built in Portland's earliest period lie within the recently created Historic District. Those that lie without — the Wadsworth-Longfellow House, for instance — are reminders of the late eighteenth and early nineteenth century styles that at one time dominated the central part of the peninsula, but now exist only in isolated pockets.

At the time of Mowatt's attack, the principal settlement of Falmouth Neck was bounded to the east by King (now India Street) and to the west by Love Lane (now Center Street). Fore Street actually ran easterly of King and continued well along toward Brackett Street, while the northerly boundary was Back Street, the main access to the countryside. King, Fore, Middle, Back, Franklin, Pearl, Fish (now Exchange), Plum and Temple Streets were lined with houses, shops and offices, the greatest concentration being on King and Middle Streets. Nearly three-quarters of this area was destroyed and significant rebuilding did not commence until after the Revolutionary War.

The flavor of local pride in the community's progress and architecture (as well as righteous anger at Mowatt), is revealed in excerpts of a letter written in 1775 by the Reverend Samuel Deane, who succeeded Parson Smith.

Reverend Samuel Deane

"Sir—I find you have been so partial to me as to manifest in a letter to the Col. some opinion of my skill in drawing, by desiring that I would suggest some alterations and amendments in Pointer' draft (of a map). I profess but little experience in such matters; but I have been examining it as well as I could—and in general I think the design very badly executed; for I can find scarcely one building drawn according to truth. King Street is not so straight as it ought to have been; and all the houses adjoining it are drawn with their ends to the street, whereas the most of them fronted it. The court-house is miserably done . . . Barns and buildings of less importance are almost wholly omitted, and some large stores not inserted. All the buildings between the wind-mill and Fiddle Lane on Back Street are left out. These are some of the most essential faults that have occurred to me; but it would be endless to enumerate all the errors.

I should think it advisable that the gentleman who makes the plate should come and see the town . . . But if it should be thought best to go on with the work immediately, I would suggest the following alterations:

Let barns, &c., be placed where you can recollect there were any; and perhaps it would not be amiss to make some where you do not remember any. Not only does justice require it, but it is necessary to give the appearance of a compact settlement. Let the meeting-house have a bell, and also a window or two in the tower. Especially let the taking of a man with a torch in Cox's lane be inserted. The stripping of a fallen officer near to Capt. Pearson's house in the street; and the knocking down of an incendiary with the breech of a gun near to Mr. Butler's door . . .

The wharves should be nearer paralell with the cross streets than they are . . . The hill at the north-east end of the Neck is not near high enough; nor do the grave-stones appear plenty enough in the burying ground. The land should rise, you know, as you come out of the town; from Capt. Joseph McLellan's to Mr. Joshua Brackett's, it is up-hill . . .

At the bottom you may put something like the following:— "that execrable scoundrel and monster of ingratitude, Capt. H. Mowatt, of Scotland, who had been treated with extraordinary kindness a few months before by the town of Falmouth, obtained by his most earnest solicitation an order from Graves, one of King George's admirals lying at Boston, together with the command of a small fleet, having on board the necessary apparatus, to burn and destroy the said town . . . And this just view of the town in flames, is made public to shew to the world a specimen of the conduct of George the third and his tory-underlings, towards colonists who were supposed to be uneasy under British tyranny; and what vengeance was executed upon them long before the corrupt court of Britain declared them to be a state of rebellion.

If you do not like the words execrable scoundrel, you may say, infamous incendiary, or what you please.

Your humble servant,

Samuel Freeman, Esq.   SAMUEL DEANE

The post-Revolutionary period saw the expansion of the city in all directions. Present-day India, Congress and Middle Streets had been laid out in 1724; but High, Park and Spring Streets were not built until 1788, and Danforth in 1792. Construction of three new or extended wharves was begun in 1793 by the proprietors of the adjacent Fore River flats. Between 1796 and 1823 four bridges were built connecting the Neck to its near neighbors. One of these, Vaughan's Bridge, was planned by William Vaughan who owned four hundred acres on Bramhall Hill. Before it could be developed, Vaughan was forced to sell after the 1807 Embargo Act ruined him. As the city gradually developed westward, another land entrepreneur, John Bundy Brown, acquired much of the Vaughan tract. Brown and his heirs insisted on a high standard of residential environment, reflected today in the area's gracious atmosphere.

104

LOCAL LATE COLONIAL

It was on the tide of an economic boom, then, that General Peleg Wadsworth built the first brick dwelling on the peninsula in 1785. His choice of a site at 487 Congress Street, (fig. 1), just west of Center Street, was considered a bold move out from the city's residential nucleus. With two loads of brick shipped from Philadelphia, his original two and one-half story dwelling was completed in 1786.

A nineteenth century conjectural drawing of Wadsworth's home (fig. 2), and the Captain Nathaniel Dyer House, another early brick structure, give some sense of the original proportions of the house before the addition of a third story and the

2. *House as it appeared in 1786*

105

3. *Captain Nathaniel Dyer House 1803*

front portico. Architecturally, the house is significant for its greatly simplified late Georgian vocabulary; a projecting string-course separating first and second stories, and the gently arched window and (originally) door openings.

Common to this early group is a symmetrical floor plan with rooms laid out to either side of an entrance hall containing the staircase. The regularity of the ground plan is reflected in the elevation which reveals on the first story a center doorway flanked by two windows on each side. This placement of openings is repeated on the second story.

Captain Nathaniel Dyer's needs were more modest. In 1803, he chose a site at 168 York Street (fig. 3) near the water, his source of income. Although the façade has an equal number of openings, they are smaller and closer together. The house is two narrow bays deep, resulting in its tall slender appearance. A similar vertical delicacy is obvious in the doorway. A projecting wood cornice, supported by two pilasters enframes the door and its charming semi-circular fanlight.

Sometime in the 1790's on the newly laid-out Pleasant Street, a number of similar dwellings were erected. The home of Thomas Skelton built about 1798, erroneously thought to be that of John Masury, (fig. 4), which until recently stood at Number 82, is a frame version of the local late Colonial style. In its restoration, (fig. 5), at a new site on Route One in

106

4. Thomas Skelton House c. 1798
82 Pleasant Street

Falmouth, the asphalt siding has been removed and the clapboard siding restored to match the authentic original window moldings, the cornice and pilasters of the entranceway, and the unusually large central chimney.

5. Thomas Skelton House.
Now at 124 U.S. Route 1, Falmouth
National Register of Historic Places 1973

6. *Daniel How House 1799*
    National Register of Historic Places 1973

Within a few years many other houses appeared on this street. Daniel How, a hatter and successful merchant, was attracted from Standish in 1799 to the growing bustle of Portland. His substantial brick residence at 23 Danforth Street, (fig. 6), one of the city's first ten brick dwellings, backed on Pleasant and was close above the water on Danforth Street.

Although a frame structure, the house built the following year at 127 Pleasant Street, (fig. 7), by Thomas Delano is amazingly like the How House in plan and elevation, except for the added portico. One important difference is the location of the fireplaces. As the chimneys indicate, those of the How House are on the exterior walls, while Thomas Delano's were placed on the interior walls which separate front from back rooms.

7. *Thomas Delano House 1800*

109

8. McLellan-O'Toole House 1813

Park Street, developed as Ann Street in 1785 by Thomas Robison, comprised part of a large tract extending from Congress Street to the waterfront and contained a ropewalk, wharf, distillery and two dwellings, one at either end. By the time of the building of the McLellan-O'Toole House at 57 Park Street in 1813, (fig. 8), several more dwellings ran the length of this street. The period of its full development was to come some twenty years later.

In this earlier group of buildings, the McLellan-O'Toole House is unusual but not unique. The structure combines stylistic elements from two periods. The principal entrance was originally a broad fanlighted door of the Federal type (fig. 9) instead of the later (but curiously more eighteenth century) enclosed portico seen today. The lovely entranceway of the ell is quite similar to the doors of the How and Dyer Houses; the almost flat hipped roof must have been influenced by the more elaborate homes built between the Wadsworth-Longfellow House and this structure.

This influence was certainly clear when the Wadsworth-Longfellow House was rebuilt in 1815. The addition of a third story with its flatter roof design and the resultant heightening and elongation of proportions marked the shift even more clearly from late Colonial to the new Federal style.

9. McLellan-O'Toole House with fan-lighted door

111

THE FEDERAL STYLE: REFINEMENT

The economic momentum that followed the Revolution culminated architecturally in a series of handsome Federal mansions built for merchants, shippers and professional men who had made fortunes during this period. The lasting impression of this building period (1784 to about 1815) is noted by William Willis in his 1849 edition of the *Journals of the Reverend Thomas Smith and the Reverend Samuel Deane.* He says: "this year (1800) commenced the erection of costly and beautiful mansions; . . . (they) were objects of great attraction in their day as specimens of substantial workmanship and handsome style of architecture . . . And now, at the end of half a century, few dwelling houses are superior to them either in style or solidity."

Of the seven large dwellings built on High Street between Congress Square and Danforth Street during the years 1800 to 1807, those of Hugh McLellan, (fig. 10), now the McLellan-Sweat Mansion, and Stephen McLellan, (fig. 11), now the Cumberland Club at 116 High Street, still dominate the neighborhood. The two brothers, shippers and importers, commissioned a local masterbuilder, John Kimball, senior, to design these two handsome houses.

John Kimball owned a fine library of builders' manuals, a sure eye and a lively imagination. He combined these assets to produce, for example, the stunning Palladian windows on the second story over the entranceway.

These graceful openings, a central arched light flanked by two narrower pilastered sections, carry upward the emphasis made by the projecting entrance porticos. Typically, a Federal house has a full three-story elevation, terminating in a shallow hipped roof and often surmounted by a wooden balustrade, as in the Hugh McLellan Mansion and originally in Stephen McLellan's. The delicacy of the balustrade is repeated in the tall Doric columns of the portico and the lovely hand carved urns of the original fence.

113

The ground story windows in both dwellings were lengthened in the 1820's by Charles Quincy Clapp. This modification, together with the deep window cornices, emphasizes the feeling of height so readily apparent in the high-ceilinged interiors.

The English prototypes illustrated in builders' books were usually of stone with its attendant solidity and formality. American builders found similar ways to enhance their brick or frame structures. Hence, like the Hugh McLellan Mansion, many brick houses were painted. Or, in the case of the frame Matthew Cobb Mansion (fig. 12), once on the site of the Libby Building at the corner of High and Congress Streets, the boards were laid flush. Nathan Goold's father, William, noted in 1816: ". . . Its unsullied white front, with no sign of joint or seam, gave it the appearance of being cut from an immense block of statuary marble, leaving the carved ornaments standing out in relief . . ." Nathan Goold inherited from his father a love of architecture. An antiquarian and librarian of the Maine Historical Society at the beginning of this century, he wrote numerous informative articles on old Portland buildings that provide invaluable insights into the city's concern for her heritage.

12. Matthew Cobb Mansion 1801, Alexander Parris

115

15. *Ingraham House in 1948*

While lots were being sold and buildings erected on High Street, Joseph Holt Ingraham, a merchant and land developer, was foresighted enough to buy large tracts of land to the west, beyond Park Street. In 1800, he began to plat State Street. Ingraham, who also opened Market Street from Middle to Fore Streets, was a representative to the General Court and a Portland selectman. Earlier in 1777, he had built the first house after Mowatt's raid and in 1801 commissioned the young Alexander Parris to design his new house at 51 State Street (fig. 13). Originally it was quite similar to the destroyed Matthew Cobb Mansion (also attributed to Parris); but it is apparent that the architect evolved different solutions for the articulation of the basically rectangular mass. In both he used wooden pilasters to define and heighten the façades. In the Cobb House four of them extended from the basement, but in the

116

16. Ingraham House in 1972

Ingraham mansion he used six, rising from a slender horizontal base above the ground story windows. By doing this he unified the second and third stories into a monumental block, leaving the lowest story as a solid "basement" to the more delicately ordered upper portion.

As in the McLellan Houses, there is a handsome fan lighted doorway, but in place of their second story Palladian windows, Parris, who worked with John Kimball during his brief stay in Portland, designed a three-part, second story window and an arched third story central opening, a subtle heightening consonant with the pilaster system. Successive transformations, unhappily, have obliterated the original clapboards and the lovely pilasters, destroying the authentic elegance of the original design (figs. 14, 15, 16).

14. Ingraham House in early 1920's

117

17. Richard Hunnewell House 1805,
   Alexander Parris
   National Register of Historic Places 1973

118

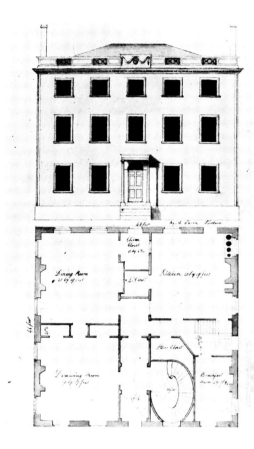

With the Ingraham House as an example, lots on State Street were in great demand. In 1804 Richard Hunnewell bought his parcel from Ingraham and, like him, commissioned Parris to design his new house which was built the following year (fig. 17). Hunnewell, who had participated in the Boston Tea Party when he was fourteen, was High Sheriff of Cumberland County from 1809 to 1811 and from 1812 to 1821.

In spite of changes made by the successive owners, this Federal mansion resembles those designed by John Kimball more than the other Parris buildings. Between 1837 and 1877, during the ownership of Ether Shepley and, later, his son, General George Shepley, both eminent jurists, interior and exterior modifications were made. In the 1920's, after acquisition by the Portland Club, John Calvin Stevens I restored the structure and added the Palladian window, the front entrance and the portico.

The Prentiss Mellen House at 166 State Street (fig. 18) went up next to the Hunnewell place in 1807. Mellen, a United States Senator and first Chief Justice of Maine, built a rather more blocky brick structure. Without a central entrance the street façade seems simpler. Although the present porch is not original, the side entrance gives a pleasing horizontal extension. In any event, the solution of using a side entrance occurred frequently in Portland, and in this instance varies the rhythms of State's monumental streetscape.

Mellen weathered the Embargo Act. After a series of ownerships the house was sold in 1848 to William Pitt Fessenden, United States Senator and one time Secretary of the Treasury. The merchant builders of Federal mansions fared worse; both McLellans and Joseph Ingraham lost their homes. What probably cost between $15,000 and $20,000 to build were sold at greatly depressed prices in 1807 and the years following. The Ingraham dwelling was acquired in 1816 by William Pitt Preble for $3,665, and Asa Clapp bought the Hugh McLellan place for $4,050 in 1817.

18. Prentiss Mellen House 1807

19. McLellan-Oxnard House 1830

Doorway of above

It is not surprising, therefore, to discover how few new structures — only four in 1809 — were built after the Embargo Act; nor less surprising to find those of the next two decades considerably more modest.

Five late Federal dwellings introduced plans and building solutions which have become typical of Portland architecture. Perhaps to retain the monumentality of the grander mansions, the builders of the McLellan-Oxnard House at 94-96 Danforth Street (fig. 19), now occupied by the Catherine Morrill Day Nursery, and the Joseph How House at 30-32 Pleasant Street (fig. 20) combined two dwellings into one brick mass. The façades of these double houses are six bays (rather than five) wide, with the two entrances side by side in the center. Granite lintels in one instance, shallow brick arches in the other, cap the windows, while a diminishing upward rhythm is established by the smaller third story sash.

120

In place of the familiar central plan, these two double houses substitute a side hall plan with the principal rooms arranged economically one behind the other, rather than symmetrically off a central hall.

Doorway, John How House (fig. 23)

20. Joseph How House

121

Of significance here is a quite different aesthetic; the flat façades seem almost to hang curtain-like from the eaves, with arched openings cut out to reveal the recessed doorways. The Neal Dow House (fig. 21), built in 1829, is an exception. It does not have a recessed opening, but in common with the Bosworth Memorial (fig. 22) and the Pleasant Street house, it has a stepped gable which seems to add height while retaining a fairly deep gabled roof.

The John How House at 40 Pleasant Street (fig. 23) built behind his own dwelling by Daniel How for his son in 1817, makes an interesting comparison with the earlier house. Here the proportions are broader; the effect, as the doorways amply demonstrate, is more sculptural and less linear.

122

22.   Bosworth Memorial Hall

23.   John How House 1817

HOUSES OF WORSHIP

Of the three important public buildings of the period which remain, the First Parish Church at 425 Congress Street (fig. 24) has the longest tradition of any in Portland. The congregation was established in 1674 and the first two meeting houses were located on India Street. The present site was chosen for a new frame church – "Old Jerusalem" – in 1740. In addition to its roster of important early members which included Prentiss Mellen, William Pitt Preble, Asa Clapp, Stephen Longfellow, it was here in 1819 that the Constitution of the new State of Maine was drafted. By 1824, however, the frame structure was declared unfit and a building committee of three presented plans to the parish on March 25, 1825. A contract was signed April ninth with Nathan Howe, joiner, and Henry Dyer, mason, "to furnish material and to erect and completely furnish the house for the sum of $15,000." The dedication was held on February eighth, the following year. Remodeled in 1852, it was later changed back to its original design in 1886 and the present parish house was added in 1890.

Today the First Parish Church, like the Wadsworth-Longfellow House, provides Congress Street with an unexpected visual contrast. The church, impressively situated at the head of Temple Street, is flanked by large old trees, setting it off from its neighbors.

Stylistically, this church represents a transition from the earlier eighteenth century form of fully projecting central tower, and from the later Federal and Greek Revival structures characterized by a full portico with the tower rising from the roof, behind the entrance.

Its unusual blocky granite contrasts sharply with the rosy, gentler brick of the Park Street Church at 133 Pleasant Street (fig. 25), built in 1828. Now the Holy Trinity Hellenic Orthodox Church, it, too, exemplifies the transitional style; tower to nave softened by two lateral stepped porches; the main arched

24. *First Parish Church 1825*
   National Register of Historic Places 1973

125

25. *Park Street Church 1828*

entrances echoed in similar side doors. The arch motif is repeated in a lunette in the First Parish about half-way up the
tower and in an arched window set high above in the Park
Street Church.

The tower of the First Parish is designed handsomely in two
stages, surmounted by a balustrade to effect the transition to

126

26. *Entranceway of First Parish Church*

the octagonal domed belfry. Above this, a lantern and spire
lead the eye upward to the bannerette weathervane, saved from
"Old Jerusalem." In the Park Street Church, the shorter tower
rises in one continuous stage to a square wooden belfry which
is surmounted by a proportionately larger octagonal lantern
and spire.

127

27. *Mariner's Church 1829*
National Register of Historic Places 1973

While the dominant aesthetic of these two churches is the tower and its successful combination with entranceways and meeting area, the Mariner's Church at 366-376 Fore Street (fig. 27) presented different design problems. Dedicated in 1829, three years after the First Parish Church, it, too, has a granite façade, although the rest of the structure is brick. The trustees of the Mariner's Church had incorporated in 1827 to provide a Seamen's Chapel for the religious edification of mariners. The chapel was planned for the third story; the lower two, appropriately for the location on Fore Street, were planned for stores and "other apartments."

Its architectural scheme is similar to two well-known Massachusetts buildings: Faneuil Hall in Boston and the 1824 Peabody Museum (East India Marine Hall) in Salem. Like the former more delicate structure, the Mariner's Church façade is articulated in three stories surmounted by a gable end containing a lunette. As in the Peabody Museum (a two story façade), the Portland building has arched lights on only the second story, while the granite façades of each dictated simpler, heavier

128

decoration. It is tempting, of course, to regard the Mariner's Church as a local precursor of the Greek Revival buildings of the following decade.

Unlike some New England towns where almost entire late eighteenth and early nineteenth century sections have remained intact, Portland's particular richness derives both from the juxtaposition of many building styles and from the continued uses and associations of its structures. The Mariner's Church serves to introduce Asa Clapp, a highly successful merchant and shipowner and the father of Charles Quincy Clapp. After the panic of 1837, the trustees of the Mariner's Church were forced to sell. Asa Clapp began buying and owned the major portion by 1839. This energetic man, whose handsome Federal house once stood at the corner of Elm and Congress Streets, survived the Embargo Act and pledged an enormous amount of money to the government during the War of 1812. Both Presidents Monroe and Polk had visited his home before his death in 1848.

The Richard Hunnewell House was acquired by Nehemiah Cram in 1828. Cram, an important merchant, held the organizational meeting for the new High Street Church here in 1830. Seven years later the dwelling was bought by Ether Shepley, a former United States Senator who had, only a year earlier, been appointed to the Supreme Court of Maine. In 1848 he became Chief Justice. His son, to whom the house was conveyed in 1868, had been a brigadier general in the Civil War and was later appointed a judge of the United States Circuit Court. The present owner, the Portland Club, acquired the property in the 1920's.

The Delano dwelling on Pleasant Street was bought in 1820 by Henry Ilsley whose son Isaac, to whom it passed, was Collector of Customs. The Ilsley family in 1872 conveyed the dwelling to Nathan Webb, a notable jurist and a hospitable literary man who often entertained the Fraternity and Rossini Clubs. The structure has served since 1959 as the offices of Stevens Architects, a firm established in Portland since 1884.

REVIVAL STYLES: 1820-1866

A NATIONAL STYLE

Although the period from 1820 to 1850 did not see the amount of building activity of previous or subsequent years, it did witness the introduction of the Greek Revival, a style that considerably influenced the future look of the city.

The Greek Revival might well be called a national American style for it is found in Washington, in Louisiana, in Wisconsin, as abundantly as in New England. Nor should its symbolic value be underestimated. Late eighteenth century archaelogical discoveries and the fight for Greek independence had shifted European enthusiasms away from ancient Rome to ancient Greece. Thus the double appropriateness of ancient and modern Greek ideals recommended itself to the American democracy.

With the ancient Greek temple in its many varieties as its basis, with a rich decorative vocabulary taken from the three ancient orders – all available in European, English, and subsequently American engraved illustrated books, local architects and builders had abundant material to use.

The Charles Q. Clapp and Thomas W. O'Brion Houses, the former Engine Four Fire House and the vernacular dwelling on the northeast corner of Spring and Brackett Streets point out the universality and adaptability of the Greek Revival style in local architecture.

Charles Q. Clapp came from an enterprising family and married well. His wife, Julia Octavia Wingate, was the daughter of his father's business associate and grand-daughter of General Henry Dearborn. Like his father, Asa, who owned the Mariner's Church Building by 1844, Charles was a land and building speculator and like Thomas Jefferson, a gentleman architect. There are on record over six hundred real estate transactions involving him; he was responsible for redesigning the first-story front windows on the two McLellan Mansions, for work on the present St. Elizabeth's Home and for remodeling the Old City, or Market, Hall which stood in what is now Monument Square.

Clapp's design for his own house at 97 Spring Street (fig. 29), built in 1832, is both elegant and unusual. Instead of the conventional Greek Revival prostyle colonnade seen on the O'Brion residence, Clapp's temple façade is pseudo-peripteral, consisting of a pediment, Ionic entablature and six-fluted columns. The cella has been pulled forward as another support for the pediment, and is handsomely enframed by fluted Ionic pilasters. This treatment emphasizes the vertical thrust, as does the rising ground of the site and the high, stone granite basement. Urns once crowned the three pedestals still visible at the ends and apex of the front and rear pediments.

By comparison, the O'Brion home (fig. 30), built fifteen years later in 1847 at 172 State Street next to the Prentiss Mellen House and subsequently owned briefly by Clapp, is less thoughtfully proportioned. The broader pediment is supported by an entablature and five Ionic columns, spaced to emphasize the side entrance and its balancing counterpart which were placed only two columns back, rather than the three of the earlier dwelling.

Detail: Spring Street Firehouse

134

31. Spring Street Firehouse 1837

Modern changes have had more obvious effect here than on the Clapp residence. The dark grey pediment sits too heavily on the still-handsome white columns and the ersatz vestibule bears no relationship to the original design.

What is obvious in these dwellings, in the Fire House and in the modest vernacular house on Spring and Brackett Streets, is an aesthetic which relies on strength rather than delicacy. In the Fire House, a modification of the temple façade is obvious in the broad pediment, supported in this instance by four pilasters rising from a low stringcourse separating the basement story (fig. 31). The use of heavy granite blocks in the façade of this brick building is typical of the heavier proportions of the Greek Revival.

135

32. *Mid-nineteenth century double dwelling 207-209 Spring Street*

Situated between the mansions of State Street and High Street and the row house development of Park Street, this building was erected by the city in 1837 as a combination firehouse, school and voting place. The school continued until 1869; the other two functions were maintained until 1966.

The modest frame structure at 207-209 Spring Street (fig. 32), two-tenths of a mile west of the Fire House, is representative of the development of the city westward between State and Emery Streets, and between York and Congress Streets. The area is spotted with nicely proportioned late Greek Revival single and multiple dwellings, though later refurbishments have obscured their handsomer details. Fitting rather snugly between these are other later dwellings of craftsmen, tradesmen, and workingmen, equally interesting as apt modifications of high styles.

The Spring - Brackett Streets house also demonstrates the importance of a high basement, here worked in brick, as a

136

33. A later nineteenth century residence, 22 Spruce Street

stylistic feature. The upper frame part was until recently nicely outlined by modified corner pilasters and a wide entablature on the principal façade. The entrance is recessed and crowned by a heavy lintel; the windows were once capped by handsome moldings, features adapted from grander masonry structures and found in other modest Greek Revival buildings.

The influence of this rather severe, forthright style continued for many years, as is apparent at 22 Spruce Street (fig. 33). The high pitch of the gable, the bracket decoration and projecting bay are clues to a late nineteenth century date, but the window framing, corner pilasters and doorway are comfortable, time-tested stylistic features from an earlier era.

Spruce Street looking west

34. Old City or Market Hall,
Market Square

Although few examples remain, the "temple" style of Greek Revival architecture was once an important visual factor in the Portland scene. The Old City Hall in Market Square (fig. 34) (now Monument Square), was an original John Kimball Jr. design modified by Charles Clapp in 1833 with the addition of a columned portico and the removal of a cupola into the more massive and severe Greek Revival.

The Exchange (fig. 35), begun in 1836, finished in 1839 and

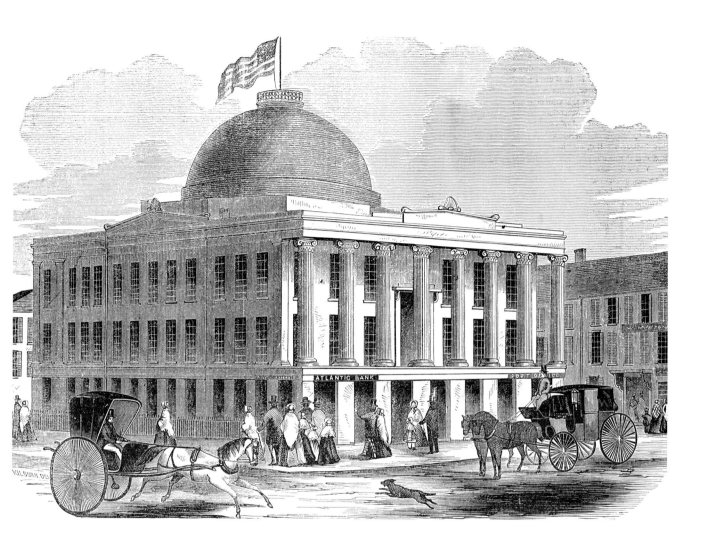

burned in 1854, once stood at Middle and Exchange Streets. Its seventy-two foot façade consisted of a high basement story supporting a two story Ionic colonnade. The length on Exchange Street was one hundred thirty-six feet and the whole was surmounted by a shallow dome sixty-three feet in diameter. Thus the popular gathering place in Market Square and the center of the business district were characterized by the solid formality of this truly national style.

35. Exchange Building 1836-1854
Middle and Exchange Streets

139

36. *John Neal Houses*
1836

ROW HOUSES: AN URBAN SOLUTION

Four years after Clapp finished his imposing townhouse, another building went up, designed by an even more controversial gentleman architect. The duplex at numbers 173 and 175 State Street (fig. 36) was erected in 1836 under the direction of John Neal. Neal was born in Portland in 1793. By the time he was twenty-four, he had failed in business and had written his first novel, *Keep Cool.*

140

Neal was a prolific writer, well-informed critic, a generous patron. He loved his native city. His *Portland Illustrated*, published in 1874, two years before his death, reveals an affectionate and controversial involvement with the life of this city. It offers the modern reader a rewarding and lively look at what Portland was like to a keen-minded and sensitive nineteenth century citizen.

His original plan called for a row of eight houses to be erected on twenty-six and one-half foot by one-hundred foot lots. Neal, to his outspoken annoyance, lost investors to the competing Park Street development, and was forced to modify his plan to the handsomely severe duplex seen today.

A quick comparison of the two projects tells much of Neal and his uncompromising aesthetic standards. His duplex consists of North Yarmouth granite (from a quarry bought for that purpose), laid up in long, narrow horizontal courses, comprising a basement, with the entrance story separated from the main and two upper stories by a projecting stringcourse. The recessed entrances are enframed by Doric pilasters supporting a simple entablature and cornice. The windows directly above are set off by lateral panels and crowned by a raised lintel. The depth and spacing of these windows and their geometric iron balconies, which often cast handsome shadows on the façade (fig. 37), mark this as the principal story above which more numerous openings, diminishing in size, create a stately staccato rhythm.

The Park Street project which rivaled John Neal's was begun in 1835 and was originally named the Ann Street Company. Four acres between Gray and Congress Streets on the site of Billy Gray's ropewalk were bought on April 14 from John C. Gray of Boston for $15,000. Forty-one shares at four hundred seventy-five dollars apiece were sold with the notion of building twenty houses, fourteen on Ann Street (88-114 Park Street), and three each on Gray and Spring Streets. Construction started that summer and the company name was changed

37. Windows and iron work, Neal Houses

38. *Park Street Row 1835-1838*
National Register of Historic
Places 1972

142

to the Park Street Proprietary (fig. 38). By October third, the walls and roofs were completed and the interiors were left to the individuals' own tastes. But the Proprietary had failed to meet payments and the units were put up for auction. Although all had been sold by 1838, some were left empty, some were used for warehousing and the lots between Spring and Congress Streets were sold off separately.

It is safe to say that today's renascence of this handsome row is much closer to the vision of the Park Street Proprietary in 1835 than the actuality in 1838. The large common park in the rear is still undeveloped, but the façades retain much architectural history, especially with some bays and porticos added later in the nineteenth century.

Like many Federal and Greek Revival townhouses in Boston, these units have a three-bay façade with side-placed entrance. The second story is the principal one, with longer windows and handsome cast iron balconies. The entrances are similar to those of the John Neal duplex: Doric pilasters, entablature and simple cornice enframing a recessed door. The brick of the building is complemented by richer brownstone lintels and door surrounds.

The row house was not exploited as extensively here as the duplex: only three others come to mind from this period, one of which is on lower Park Street. Now called Stratton Court (fig. 39), this development was formerly Park Place and was built in 1847-1848, undoubtedly as a speculative venture for more modest buyers. Nine brick units, each two bays deep and three stories tall, are set on a high basement. As the first unit demonstrates, they originally had slightly recessed entrances framed by very simplified wooden paneled pilasters, lintel and an almost flattened pediment. The windows may have been much longer, and modern standard parts necessitated their unfortunate diminution. It is also possible that the lower wooden panels used in place of complete glazing, were an original economy gesture. What does remain of the original embellishments are the horizontal panels below the roof line and the cast iron foliated scrolls over many of the windows.

GOTHIC REVIVAL: DOMESTIC AND RELIGIOUS

In the late 1840's and the 1850's in the United States, a style developed which had begun in England almost a century earlier with Horace Walpole's remodeling of Strawberry Hill into a Gothic country house. The taste for the romantic revival found early and apt expression in churches like Richard Upjohn's Trinity and James Renwick's Grace Churches (both 1846) in New York City. Andrew Jackson Downing's *Country Houses*, a builders' handbook, was published in 1850 and incorporated

40. *John J. Brown House 1845, Henry Rowe*
     387 Spring Street
     National Register of Historic Places 1971

notions from English builders' books of a decade earlier. Richard Upjohn was himself an Englishman and between 1835 and 1839 had designed both a Gothic Revival church in Bangor and a dwelling called "Oaklands" in Gardiner. It is no surprise then to discover that Henry Rowe, the architect of the John J. Brown House now at 387 Spring Street (fig. 40), had English training and thus advertised himself in 1845 (fig. 41).

Gone from the Brown House are the classical details of the Federal and Greek Revival styles. In their places are tall, slender, pointed lancet windows, diamond-shaped leaded casement windows, quatrefoils and crockets and the carved foliation typical of medieval manuscript borders.

There are many fascinations in this house: it is of wood, but made to look like stone; the corners are marked by applied decorative "pier buttresses" but the building retains the four-square central plan scheme of its classical predecessors. Certainly the entrance has been pulled out into a strong projecting pavillion, allowing for a steeply pointed gable and a charming porch. The hipped portion of the roof with its fish scale-patterned slate is accordingly tall, lending to this cottage some of the much-admired soaring qualities of Gothic church architecture.

It is a pity that the unique grouping of superb Federal, Greek and Gothic Revival buildings on Spring Street has been lost by the enforced removal of the John J. Brown House (fig. 42).

On Congress and Locust Streets, approaching Munjoy Hill, sits a later Gothic cottage, originally quite similar in exterior detail to Henry Rowe's Brown House. Designed by George Pelham to adjoin the new St. Paul's Church, the rectory went up in 1869 (fig. 43). The second St. Paul's structure, built in 1802 on Church Lane between Middle and Federal Streets, had been a solid brick, late eighteenth century design with a projecting central bell tower. When it burned in 1866, the new structures were appropriately and fashionably Gothic. Today's clapboarding of the rectory is misleading and seems to be at odds with the pleasing Gothic details. The siding, like that of

41. *Henry Rowe advertisement*

42. *Gothic House in original location, 86 Spring Street*

the Gothic House, was originally wood, cut and beveled to imitate stone (fig. 44). The window moldings, steep gables and hipped roof, the crocketed corner "nook" are strongly reminiscent of the earlier structure, while the delicately-pointed arcade, supported on slender colonettes and suggesting a cloister, is unique in present day Portland.

Also of later design is the Seaman's Club Building at 375 Fore Street (fig. 45), designed and erected by Charles Clapp immediately after the fire of 1866. This and the adjacent building (now partially obscured by a large sign) are characterized

45. Seaman's Club 1866-1867

44. St. Paul's Church and Rectory,
late nineteenth century photograph

149

by broad graceful Gothic lights as well as four intertwining pointed arches topped by three medallions, all circumscribed by a gently rounded arch. While in a typical Gothic vocabulary, this broad expanse of windows anticipates later Victorian commercial façades.

The State Street Church (fig. 46), although grander in size than its neighbors, fits well the broad and generous scale of the State Street environment. The congregation, formed by a younger group in the High Street Church, raised enough money to build this structure in 1851.

The present façade is a change from the original plan. The first façade (fig. 47), dominated by a central wooden spire resting on a tower which incorporated the masonry entranceway, rose squarely to well above the gable and then narrowed into the spire which soared far above the tree tops. The design by William Washburn of Boston, although not as broad, was quite similar to Richard Upjohn's Trinity Church in New York City and typical of early Gothic Revival buildings.

Around 1871, the wooden spire which had been struck by lightning was removed; the present red freestone façade was added in 1892-1893 by John Calvin Stevens I. The sheer height has given way to breadth. The width of the gable is emphasized by the screen of three doors and by the assymmetrical flanking towers. The tall narrow façade window reflects the delicacy still visible in the original design of the north and south sides, while the heavy stone building material tells much of the aesthetic sensibilities of the late nineteenth century.

Three other State Street churches provide a nice present-day capsule of the neo-Gothic style. St. Dominic's, dedicated in 1893, is the most strongly vertical. Narrow buttresses and windows, delicate moldings and the brick itself give it a lean, ascetic look. The State Street Church seems to fit, visually, between St. Dominic's and St. Luke's Cathedral, built in 1868. The last is of tan stone and generous, blocky proportions, relating more to an earlier country Gothic than to the formality of the urban cathedral style.

*47. State Street Church 1851,
William Washburn*

151

48. *Carroll Mansion 1851*

ARCHITECTURAL DIVERSITIES
OF THE 1850's

The economic expansion and diversification of the 1850's, made tangible in the filling and development of Commercial Street, was reflected in building activity of all sorts: foundries, commercial blocks, hotels, a jail, schools, and a library. From filled land on one side of the peninsula to filled land on the other, new buildings were erected, many of which were demolished in 1965 and 1966. The original Grand Trunk Railroad Station, built below Fore and India Streets in 1856 was later replaced in 1903; and the Monroe Street Jail in Bayside was built in 1858. Between these on Congress Street, St. Stephen's Church was erected in 1854-1855. The only remaining building of this period of activity, Mechanic's Hall, also went up on Congress Street. And appropriately, the 1850's brought residential building of a scale unknown since the flourishing of Federal architecture. The Carroll Mansion on Park Street facing Danforth Street was built in 1851. Below it the Morse-Libby House was begun in 1859. William Safford's bow front house at 93 High Street (now the Portland School of Art) was built in 1858, and John Bundy Brown built his villa out from the center of town on Bramhall Hill, later to be developed as a fine residential area.

The ubiquitous Charles Q. Clapp was involved in the purchase of the property for the Carroll Mansion in 1848 (fig. 48). He paid $4500 for it and built the house for his daughter, Julia, who had married John Bryce Carroll in the First Parish Church in 1843. Carroll was a Virginian whose tobacco business brought him to Portland. His interests also included the Casco Bank and a term as a city councillor in 1856. His obituary (1868) reveals something of the graciousness of that period in Portland: "The lavish hospitality of his house, the quiet yet broad generosity of his hand, the pleasure of his companionship in the walks and ways of life, awake among us all of every station or degree the keenest regret that he is no more."

153

49. 85-87 State Street 1851

Although visually related to the earlier Federal mansions, certain significant changes in architectural thinking are here apparent. The main, solid block is finished by an Italianate frieze, cornice and slightly hipped roof. The central portal is adorned with a handsome projecting portico, a reconstruction by the present owner in 1918, fluted Ionic columns supporting a frieze and pediment. In place of the slender delicacy of the Federal style, and without the obvious temple prototype of the Greek Revival, this design has a solid massiveness which was to become more common as the century wore on. Characteristic are the grouped windows, crowned with heavy double lintels; the strongly projecting cornice; and the deep portico surmounted by a rectangular bay.

Similar in feeling and vocabulary is the handsome double house at 85-87 State Street (fig. 49), built in the same year. The continuous dormer was added much later. This structure also retains the classical frieze and cornice, supporting a pitched roof; pilasters march across the façade much as they formerly did in its neighbor, the Ingraham House; the double doors bear

154

fan lights. The deep windows are grouped, a central light flanked by narrower openings and framed by a simple but broad projecting brick band. On closer examination the fan- lights seem more generous – their hemicycles divided by mul- lions into larger sections, while the pilasters articulate the building into three clearly defined units. And finally, (in line with the changing aesthetic direction) the strongly projecting entrance portico is supported not on columns, but by deep, generous consoles.

The same motif of portico on consoles was used in the Fitch- Swan Houses at 177-179 State Street (fig. 50). Built in 1862, on property purchased from John Neal, the changes of taste are most evident. The 1850's found Boston's South End (filled land) being lined by handsome row houses with bowed fronts. The Safford House at 93 High Street earlier developed this motif in Portland, an architectural idea that continued to be used for double houses and later still, complex apartment dwellings like those on lower State and High Streets.

While the bowed façade provides the illusion, at least, of

155

more light and space on the interior of a town house, the exterior establishes a new rhythm on the streetscape. In place of the steady, measured beat of the John Neal door and window openings, the Fitch-Swan façade swells and diminishes. In the severe John Neal houses each opening has equal importance; it is the addition of single parts that make a whole. The Fitch-Swan façade is a sculpture-like entity in which single parts are subordinate to the total effect, especially when covered by its original mastic over the now visible brick. The bays swell out from the flat central area which, in turn, adds to the visual richness with deep-set portals and a projecting, shadowy, arcaded balcony above. The play of light and shade is continued in the scooped-out niches which grow less deep and visually more delicate as they go upward.

It is well to recall that in the 1850's interiors were becoming more opulent. Deep-piled, rich fabrics, curved, carved furniture, gilt and rosewood, provided visual counterpoint to the sculptural aesthetic of the exteriors.

PORTLAND'S ITALIAN VILLAS

One of the most famous interiors of this era, still intact, is at 109 Danforth Street in the Morse-Libby House (the Victoria Mansion, fig. 51) built by Ruggles Sylvester Morse, a Maine native who made his fortune in New Orleans. In deciding to build a summer home in Portland, he bought land that year from Alice Ilsley on the corner of Park and Danforth Streets, abutting the Carroll Mansion property. Directly across Danforth Street was the McLellan-O'Toole House, a frame two story structure; and directly across Park Street was the Robison-Cutter House (now the Home for the Aged), a delicately-scaled brick Federal residence. Morse's mansion even today remains unique in its grand scale. Although enhanced by generous lawns, the sheer textural ingenuity and careful feeling for architectonic massing have created the solid but varied effect of this dwelling.

157

What the exterior massing makes quite obvious is the assymetry of the ground plan despite a central hall. Instead of the simple block, central hall scheme of earlier mansions, this façade is composed of three unequal but interpenetrating blocks, an arrangement reflected in the unequal sizes and orientation of the interior spaces. The square tower rises a story above and projects a bay out from the flat-roofed rectangular mass on the west; the section on the east is stepped forward of the tower on one side, its pediment nicely overlapping at the rondel. On the other side the mass steps back and then projects again. Similarly the entrance portico, narrowed in keeping with the tower, by the placement of doubled Ionic columns, projects to support a balustraded balcony. This motif is continued on the western block after a slight setback (fig. 52). The porch thus formed is supported, appropriately, by more widely spaced Ionic columns. The greater projection of the eastern mass is emphasized by a strong rectangular bay.

The choice of building material, typical of this period, was probably made by the architect, Henry Austin, of New Haven. Shipped in a rough state from Connecticut, the blocks were finished on a Portland pier. Austin's use of the reddish brown stone allowed him to support his richness of design with the richness of color. Austin and his New Haven mentors, Town and Davis, along with other architects of this era, tried many revival styles. Often the same architect would design a Greek Revival church, a Gothic Revival dwelling and, in Austin's case, a fine Egyptian Revival cemetery gateway (in New Haven). Given this variety, it is not surprising that by the 1850's an eclectic style was emerging, called variously Tuscan Revival or Italian villa. In other words, it was not a question of using specific European buildings as prototypes, or even just one style, but it was a matter of searching the architectural attic for ideas which would create a new whole. Strictly speaking, Austin's plan is certainly not Tuscan, or even typical late Renaissance. It is a new style which belongs solidly in the nineteenth century. As much as anything, it is the strong sculptural

massing which makes this style unique. Where the Italian villa or palazzo was seemingly vast, Austin's building by contrast is neatly concentrated.

A good deal of this effect comes from the judicious harnessing of light and shadow. Austin modeled form as a sculptor might, using strongly projecting cornices, bold triangular and semi-circular pediments, richly carved consoles and balusters. Shadow and light contrast in the porches, in the deep-set window embrasures and in the steep arches of the tower. Smaller richness comes in the rusticated corners, the floral carving over the upper windows and the bold egg-and-dart motif below the attic story.

159

53. *Jonathan Hartwell Fletcher House 1870*

Giovanni Guidirini and eleven assistants created the painted decoration, while plasterers, gilders, silverers, intarsia workers and wood carvers finished the scheme. Such a monumental and expensively finished mansion provided much stylistic inspiration for subsequent building in Portland.

The Jonathan Hartwell Fletcher House was built in 1870, (fig. 53) at 366 Spring Street in the Bramhall section near the considerable mansion of his brother-in-law and business associate, Theophilus C. Hersey. Obviously more modest than the Morse-Libby Mansion, it uses much of the same architectural vocabulary. Its square brick mass is articulated vertically by rusticated corners and rusticated plaster strips which delineate the central entrance. Horizontally, a projecting brick string-course divides the first and second stories while the attic area is delicately described by framed indented brick panels. The long windows of the façade are varied in their moldings. A nice rhythm is established by the arrangement of center upper and two lower fully arched openings. The upper flanking windows and those on the sides are capped by flattened arches. The low hipped roof terminates in a projecting cornice supported on brackets, cleverly spaced to coincide with the attic panels. It is a house of careful balance and delicate proportion, though not as robust in design, perhaps, as its famous neighbor built at the same time across the street—the Israel Washburn House (fig. 54).

54. *Governor Israel Washburn House 1869-1870, attributed to Francis Henry Fassett*

VARIATIONS OF STYLE

A building of quite another sort, Mechanic's Hall, (fig. 55) at 519 Congress Street, was designed in a similar idiom by Thomas J. Sparrow, the first native Portland architect. While increasingly impressive residential structures were going up, the years before the Civil War were filled with building activity in other areas. The Maine Charitable Mechanic Association had been formed in 1815, "... an institution of a high praiseworthy character, embracing in its design that more

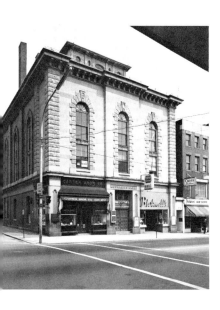

55. *Maine Charitable Mechanic's Hall
1857-1859, Thomas J. Sparrow*

elevated order of benevolence which extends its care to inform-
ing and cultivating the mind, and training up a race of
mechanics of sound moral principle and intellectual power . . ."
To this day the Association maintains a library which is still
active, sponsors lectures and a free drafting class.

In 1857 the Association voted to buy the property on Congress Street, and in 1859 the dedication was enlivened by
Daniel H. Chandler's Portland Band, one of the finest military
bands in New England.

Appropriately, Sparrow and all his workmen were members
of the Association and the architect adorned the keystones of
the high arched windows with busts of Vulcan, Archimedes and
an arm of Labor holding a sledge hammer (fig. 56).

The original plan of the building allowed for two shops on
the ground floor in front, with the back area reserved for the
Association library. This level is treated as a high basement
area with the principal floors rising in a monumental block
above, unified by the long arched windows. Those in front echo
the corner rustication in their roughened stone framing. This
strong texture is emphasized by the smoothness of the surrounding granite. While the projection of the central bay enlivens
the façade, the brick flank is articulated by pilaster strips, two
of granite and three of brick.

Elements like the rustication and the bracketed roof cornice
are common to this building and the two previous houses, yet
the architectural solution here is different. The monumental
treatment of the upper stories, where separate levels including
the severely-indented attic story are subordinated to the grand
arched scheme, sets this building apart from its neighbors.

In great contrast to the rationale of the Mechanic's Hall, the
plan of the Thomas Block on Commercial Street (fig. 57) de-
pends for its effect on long horizontal rows of shop fronts and
upper windows.

After the filling of the waterfront to create Commercial Street
in 1852, the Atlantic & St. Lawrence roundhouse and passenger

162

56. *Detail: Mechanic's Hall*

163

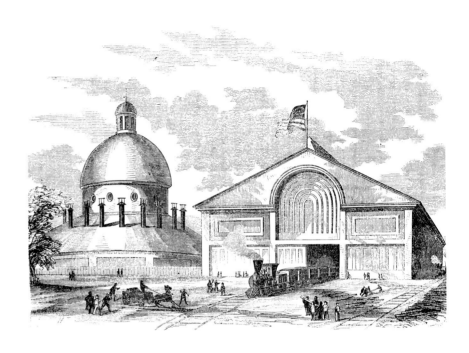

58. *Atlantic & St. Lawrence Roundhouse.*
Opened in 1855, removed 1899

station (fig. 58) were built in 1855 and 1856. Other railroads were established, wharves were built for the steamship and fishing business and a number of the present granite-faced and brick blocks were erected. The street forms an elongated S curve with the Thomas Block fitted into the area between the Customs House Wharf and Portland Pier.

William Widgery Thomas, a banker and businessman deeply involved in the development of Portland, had the block erected in 1860. The building itself presents a concave curve to the street, a motif repeated with great effect in the curved pediment which crowns the central axis.

While the Mechanic's Hall emphasizes vertical elements, the Thomas Block takes advantage of its situation on a broad, curved street. The lower floor shop fronts of nicely dressed grey

164

57. Thomas Block 1860

granite (now painted) march across the façade in an alternating rhythm of wide and narrower openings embellished by square Doric pilasters. Three stories of deep-set windows, twenty-four to a row, are embellished with granite lintels and sills. In addition, each sill and lintel rests on two small, square bracket-like granite blocks, providing nice visual relief. The projecting cornice, like that of the Mechanic's Hall, is supported by brackets separated by inset panels in the brickwork. A similar refinement embellishes the arched pediment, emphasizing the rondel

59-61. Three views of I

designed to contain a clock, since gone.

Spared by the fire of 1866, these structures and many others survive as an integral part of the city. As living archeology, they serve as a constant reminder of Portland's growth and development. Fortunately, the conflagration did not destroy the city's optimism and economic growth (fig. 59-61). In fact, as noted by John Neal, it gave businessmen and bankers the impetus to move ahead more rapidly than expected – an early case of enforced urban renewal.

ooking south; 1874, 1866, 1972

167

State Street, 1874

VICTORIAN PORTLAND: 1866-1912

"SUCCESS AND PROSPERITY"

"At the head of the table was a large joint of a la mode beef with the following inscriptions, 'Montreal Steamship Company to the U.S. Customs.' At the foot of the table was a magnificent ham, with the inscription, 'Success and prosperity to Portland' upon it. The table was literally loaded down with good things and after the company had taken their places the collector gave the word to fall to and the ravages commenced. After a lengthy struggle with the edibles, the company dispersed highly pleased with the pleasant gathering which had brought together so many of our businessmen in such an enjoyable and social manner."

So reported the *Portland Transcript* of the festivities of April 1, 1872, marking the formal opening of the new Customs House. Those present (the city government and the business community), as well as the opulence and optimism of the occasion, were appropriate to both the new building and the prevailing mood in Portland.

171

Detail: balustrade, cast iron

With the old downtown already in growing need for expansion and buildings, the fire changed its character decisively from a mixed residential and commercial area to an exclusive business community.

By the time of the fire, the customs, post office and courts in the severely damaged federal building were sorely pressed for space. It was decided to erect two new federal structures: one for the post office and courts on the site of the former building; and another to house the customs separately nearer the waterfront on bustling Commercial Street.

AFTER THE FIRE: A NEW LOOK

Although it is uncertain who designed the stately, columned "Old Post Office Building" (destroyed for the present parking lot in 1965), Alfred B. Mullett was responsible for Portland's new Customs House (fig. 62). It was the practice until early in the twentieth century for major federal buildings outside as well as within Washington to be designed by the Office of Supervising Architect of the Treasury Department, which Mullett directed.

Mullett's practice coincided both with the widespread post-Civil War rush of building activity and with the development in this country of the Baroque Revival style (sometimes referred to as Second Empire and Victorian). Certainly his most impressive structure extant is the Old State, War and Navy Building which rises in grey solidity next to the White House. It is a tribute to Mullett's architectural versatility that the much smaller Portland Customs House manages so successfully to express the monumental opulence of this era in a scale suited to its surroundings.

The site, using the block between Pearl and Custom House Streets, slopes down from Fore to Commercial Street, allowing the architect a full three-story principal façade on the waterfront with an equally handsome two-story façade on Fore Street.

172

63. *Samuel and Andrew Spring Mansions*
1854-1855, Charles A. Alexander

What could have been an awkward problem has been solved well in terms of the site and the building itself. The taller elevation with its tower serves as a focal point for the blocky three- and four-story buildings of Commercial Street, while the lower Fore Street elevation punctuates the view of Boothby Square with its smaller structures.

174

Familiar architectural elements are used – columns, arches, pediments, rustication and balustrades. But the manner in which they are organized creates a quite new effect. The engaged columns are almost fully round, the pilasters are not mere strips, but project strongly, while the double arches push the generous windows and doors more deeply into the building. The combination of substantial forms and sculptural projection invites a maximum play of light and shade. The aggressive and restless strength of the Customs House contrasts with earlier structures like the Morse-Libby House and Mechanic's Hall. In those buildings more planar areas and thinner members contribute to a feeling of verticality. The Customs House is larger, but its division vertically into strongly marked stories and horizontally into deep sculptural bays emphasizes robustness, rather than a leaner height.

The square towers on both façades reinforce and extend upward the central focus of the entrance bays. While the bays themselves are projected outward, the towers are set back in line with the balustrade, providing dynamic balance to the building.

One of the fascinations of Portland architecture is the play between large, high-style buildings like the Customs House, and less demanding but equally fashionable structures like the Spring Mansions, 300 and 308 Danforth Street (fig. 63), at the corner of Emery Street.

Samuel and Andrew Spring, uncle and nephew, had an export-import business which shipped lumber to Buenos Aires and brought wool and hides back to Portland. Andrew was living in Portland in 1854 and the partners built their twin houses by 1855, having established themselves in the prospering business community in railroads and banking as well as in shipping.

By this time Danforth Street, laid out in 1792, had been extended from Park to Brackett by 1831. In 1847 old Bridge Street, which ran from Brackett to Vaughan Street, was incorporated into it.

Perched on the steep embankment above what is now West Commercial Street, the houses, designed by Charles A. Alexander, looked out to the Fore River. On the street side they faced the Storer and Hersey Mansions which, along with three much smaller structures, occupied the then unbroken area from Emery to Vaughan and from Danforth to Spring Streets.

The strictures of size and material notwithstanding, these are impressive dwellings. The eye is led to formal entranceways by the generous granite balustrades, running along the sidewalk and turning in to frame a broad flight of granite steps. Both entrance pavillions project the full height and are terminated by pediments — one triangular, the other rounded. The upward thrust of the central portion is continued in the strongly profiled hexagonal cupolas. Unlike the Customs House, but more appropriately for these square buildings, the semi-towers are placed in the middle of the hipped roofs.

Although brick does not allow for the sort of columns and some of the other bold devices of the Customs House, it can be used to create vivid baroque effects. Brick worked to simulate stone around the doors and brick quoins at the corners, paneled pilasters, deeply grooved window moldings, strong stringcourses separating stories, and sculptural chimneys attract the play of light and shade across these lively surfaces in a way quite as attractive as the Customs House. Originally the brick on both houses was painted a uniform grey, thus minimizing the brick in favor of a more unbroken granite-looking surface.

There are many enjoyments in these houses. A walk past is rewarded by a look at the variations of window treatment in the two, or a glimpse at the charming arcaded rear portions facing each other over the grassy plot between.

THE MANSARD STYLE

Similarly, there are many interesting details in the Woodman (now called Cook, Everett and Pennell) Building, at the

177

64. *Woodman Building 1867,*
    George M. Harding
    National Register of Historic Places 1972

corner of Middle and Pearl Streets (fig. 64). Over the center
window of the second story are two plaques, one bearing the
name, "Woodman," and the one above "A.D. 1867." On the
corner at street level, forming the plinth of a cast iron column
support appears another name, "Geo. M. Harding, Architect."

George W. Woodman, who had come to Portland as a young
man in 1836, had a well-established dry goods business which
was destroyed by the fire. Surely among the first to build anew,
he created a block whose architectural atmosphere influenced
the rebuilding of the downtown and still dominates its
neighborhood.

Woodman's architect, George Harding, was one of an impressive group who helped create Victorian Portland. He was
responsible as well for the Portland High School (his portion
now obscured on the exterior) and the recently destroyed First
Universalist Church on High Street at Congress Square.

The demands Harding had to meet differed greatly from
those of Mullett in the Customs House. While the identity of a
federal building with classical forms (however combined) was
the rule until much too recently, a business block could and
did make a prosperous impression by combining necessary size
with a fashionable façade. Harding's problem, then, became
one of designing an exterior which enlivened the basic commercial block.

Marking the corners by mansard towers, (identifiable with
those of the Customs House), and emphasizing the center of each
façade by bolder fenestration and projections on the roof level,
give a sense of nicely juxtaposed masses rather than one large
block. The progression upwards of extremely tall first story
openings, elongated second and third story windows, the steep
mansard roof and the towers, provides a strongly vertical balance for the brick block.

Although there is little bold projection to catch the light,
Harding wisely used contrasting materials for the door and
window moldings, the stringcourses and the roof. In fact, the
paired colonettes and flattened arches of the street level are of

179

cast iron and usually textured with sand in the paint to simulate stone. Obviously, ornamental detail like the capitals, the keystones and the scrolls in the spandrels, is more easily and economically produced by casting than by carving.

The rebuilding of the downtown provided architectural impetus in other areas of the peninsula. Shortly after the completion of the Woodman Building, a residence at 61 Deering Street (fig. 65) was built by William H. Anderson, but was acquired less than five years later by James Phinney Baxter who, in his six terms as mayor, did much to advance the city's growth.

Before 1852, Deering Street did not exist. That year, it was laid out between High and State Streets, then extended to Mellen Street in 1858. The slight rise of the Baxter site is used advantageously to provide pleasingly broad flights of steps to the entrance. Although presently marred by a fire escape, the projecting pavillion, punctuated by a tall, slender portico and a two level tower, echoes the vertical thrusts of the Woodman Building. In addition, the steep mansard roof and the tall, narrow, paired windows are marks of an aesthetic noticeably different from that of the Spring mansions. Strong sculptural effects have been replaced by more slender proportions and decorative touches. The corners are accented by very narrow pilasters, decorated with a cast iron scroll design. The central tower is crowned by fancy iron work reminiscent of a French chateau.

The components of the mansard style are endlessly adaptable. Frame versions of this style line many of the peninsula's streets. The verticality and slenderness translate well into wood. A less generous ground plan often dictates a side hall and entrance rather than a central plan. The entranceway is more modest and the projecting bay moved to the other half of the façade as may be seen on eight Cushman Street (fig. 66).

Happily, the style can be unusually effective in row houses, as in those of 33-39 Deering Street (fig. 67). Built contemporaneously with the Baxter Mansion, this block is handsomely

181

66. *Mansard Style Residence,*
Eight Cushman Street

proportioned. Given the horizontal expanse necessary for a four-entrance façade, the design must offer a counter balance. Two devices, particularly, provide the needed vertical accents. The mansard roof, which tapers in while providing a spacious upper story, continues and resolves the upward thrust of the rustication. These rusticated pilasters, in turn, play two more roles. They project from the plain brick surface while rhythmically marking off the window and door bays. Finally, it is the proportion of first story to second story to mansard roof, each level punctuated by generous windows, that gives the row its handsome aspect.

182

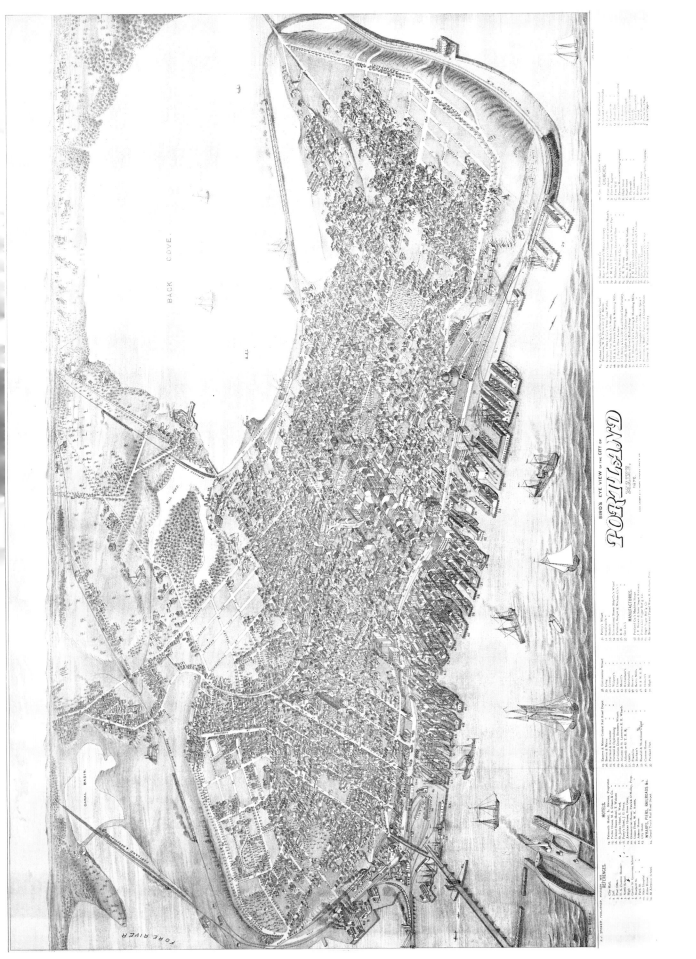

COMMERCIAL EXPANSION

One of the most extensive and important post-fire rebuilding projects was Exchange Street. Laid out in 1724 between Fore and Middle Streets, it was first called Fish Street. It retained this name until 1810. In 1793 the present extension to Congress Street was laid out as Court Street, which was changed to Exchange in 1837.

Since much of the city's business vitality was centered on Exchange, John Neal was impressed (and relieved) at its rebuilding. In 1874, he wrote:

> "We have now along both sides of this attractive and busy thoroughfare, large, handsome blocks and warehouses, of granite, iron, Albert-stone, pressed brick and common brick, three and four stories high, with mansard roofs, and large halls and chambers, adapted to the wants of a manufacturing region.
>
> These buildings are all, upon the average, fifty or sixty feet to the eaves, well-slated roofs, large, dry and well-lighted cellars, deep drainage, and generally water-closets, sinks and Sebago water; and also – a fact worth recording – with a reasonable amount of architectural embellishment, heavy cornices, rich windows, and pilasters to correspond. Instead of being only thirty-five or forty feet in depth, most of these are from eighty to one hundred and twenty, or even here and there, one hundred and fifty feet in depth, and they are generally finished within, after a superior style, with our richest native woods, black and yellow ash, maple and walnut, oiled and varnished. The floors are laid with southern pine, the cellars with heavy plank or cemented, and all are now occupied for banking-houses, brokers' offices, insurance-offices, auction-rooms, bookstores, warehouses and manufactories.
>
> The ground floor is almost always stuccoed, the ceilings frescoed, with handsome cornices, and the windows of large plate-glass.
>
> But enough may be seen at a glance, to satisfy all that a wonderful improvement in the style of architecture, and in all the ornamentation, has taken place, to say nothing of the great additional conveniences, the greater safety — not a single wooden building is there now on the street, nor in the neighborhood . . . and the Sebago water, which goes up almost of itself to the mansard roofs and attics of our highest buildings."

This was written to contrast with Neal's description of the area before the fire when he used phrases like "unpretending, moderate in size," "useless garrets," "plain to ugliness, and without ornamentation or embellishment of any kind."

The narrow, lower section slopes down rather steeply from Middle to Fore Streets, capped until recently at its upper end by an impressive civic building (the Exchange, then the Old Post Office) and bordered at its foot by the venerable Hall and Hall Building. Its narrow, enclosed quality creates an intimate exchange between the tightly spaced buildings. Although there are many similarities between them, each has very individual characteristics.

Of these, numbers 41 through 49 (fig. 68) in the upper part of the block above Milk Street, comprise a row of four stores built by Nathaniel Deering in 1867 on land owned by the heirs of Commodore Preble. Although, like the Woodman Building, this block is of four stories, its scale is smaller, appropriate to the Exchange Street site. The four first-floor shop fronts alternate wide display windows with tall, deep entrance recesses. Holding it together, both literally and visually, are two horizontal, studded iron beams which meet a granite lintel in the center over the stair door to the upper floors.

The brick of the second and third stories, once completely mastic covered, is relieved by four rusticated pilasters and enlivened by the strongly-molded curves of the arched windows. On the third story, elongated keystones tie the windows to the cornice above. It is the attic story, where the deeply-pedimented windows project boldly from the mansard roof, that pleased John Neal.

Across the street, below the Widgery Block and opposite the Stanton Block, at 34 Exchange Street, stands the former Board of Trade Building (fig. 69) once occupied by the Merchants National Bank. Built during the same time, it is both smaller and more formal.

The Board of Trade had been incorporated in 1854:

". . . to give tone and energy to the various branches of trade, and

186

68. *Commercial Row 1867,*
    41-49 Exchange Street

69. *Board of Trade Building*
    1866-1867, Matthew Stead

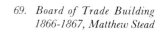

in securing the advantages which the position of the city offers to commerce and manufactures . . . and where legislation is required in making such improvements, direct its efforts in a firm and vigorous manner . . . so as to give the fullest development to all the natural advantages of the port, and provide for speedy and ample transportation of merchandise throughout the State . . . to facilitate in every possible way encouragement of commerce, and to prevent discrimination to our disadvantage in the movement of merchandise on the sea, or on the land . . ."

Its former headquarters on the same Exchange Street site was destroyed in the fire along with the original records. Early in 1868 the Board of Trade, the Merchants National Bank, the Bank of Portland and the National Traders Bank became co-tenants in the Matthew Stead-designed building.

The contrast in requirements and public image between a business block and a banking structure is apparent. Horizontal breadth to accommodate store fronts gives way to a more architecturally formal design in this, the only stone building in a brick neighborhood. If the unfortunate and intrusive coat of white paint covering and visually severing the first story, were removed, and if the now lost roof line balustrade were replaced, this building's handsome, arched rhythms would be more apparent. The alternation of large and small openings, single or clustered, the three bay definition by rusticated pilasters, the unusual shell motif in the second story windows and countless other decorative details, bespeak the aura of conservative prosperity so important to banks and boards of trade.

*Twin building, across
from the Printers' Exchange*

In the upper block of Exchange on the corner of Federal Street, stands the survivor of a pair of twin buildings (fig. 70), until recently Dow and Pinkham at 103-107 Exchange Street. These two buildings must have formed a gracious entranceway to the busy block which included the former Portland Savings Bank and, at the Middle Street corner, the Old Post Office.

Originally, Dow and Pinkham was the Printers' Exchange and housed the *Daily Argus* (Democratic), the *Daily Press* (Republican), *Zion's Advocate* (a Baptist weekly), and the *American Citizen*. Other newspapers and periodicals were pub-

189

lished on nearby Congress Street and on lower Exchange Street.

Corner buildings have a natural advantage over those which find themselves in the middle of blocks. They can command their surroundings and provide their own focal point, however modest they may be.

Here the corner is nicely designed and emphasized by its rounded shape, handsome arched window and the narrow projecting flanking strips which terminate in brackets supporting the cornice.

Although the architect is unknown and the building unpretentious, it has a handsome rightness of much the same quality as the row houses on Deering Street. There is the same neat proportion of first story to second story to hipped-roof story, the last being punctuated by round pedimented dormers. Below, the arched windows are divided into two arched lights each, the space above being filled by a circular carved decoration.

The window mullions and moldings, now painted white, contrast sharply with the red brick building. Originally, the brick, as in countless other buildings of the period, was covered by painted mastic to simulate stone. The window surrounds were undoubtedly of the same color.

THE FASSETT TRANSITION

When John Neal's *Portland Illustrated* was published in 1874, Francis H. Fassett had already established his reputation as a gifted architect. Neal wrote: "The two Fassetts, Francis H., and Edward, — father and son — with Harding, are all we have to depend on among our townsmen, chiefly for architectural embellishment." Included in the engravings of Neal's valuable book are at least eight Fassett-designed structures. By the time of his death in 1908, Fassett had provided Portland with innumerable buildings, most of which stand today as important aspects of the visual environment.

Fassett was born in Bath in 1823, served an apprenticeship to a carpenter, learned draughtsmanship and subsequently studied

architecture in Boston and New York. He came to Portland in 1863. By 1868 it was obvious he was to remain and that year he bought the parcel of "land on the Northeasterly corner of Pine and Carleton" (at 117-119 Pine Street) from John B. Brown and Philip H. Brown. In 1876 he was able to take time from his flourishing practice to build his own dwelling (fig. 71), a fine double house which terminates the vista up Thomas Street.

71. Francis H. Fassett Residences 1876

191

72. *John B. Brown Memorial Building 1882-1883, Fassett & Stevens*

Stylistically, Fassett's earlier Portland work is transitional between Mansard and Queen Anne, although later buildings fit in with the Romanesque and Classical Revival styles of the end of the century.

While his residence has a steep roof, central tower with lacy iron work and tall thin windows comparable to the Baxter House, the total effect is much more linear. The roof line as it rises, for instance, is not curved but sharply straight. Tall pointed gables, terminating the projecting window bays, flank the central tower mass. In place of the rather blocky generosity of the earlier building, here the architect has broken up the

192

mass into several strongly vertical rather than broad horizontal areas.

There is much linear decoration and a great deal of it specifically Gothic in character: the slender colonnettes supporting the entrance portico, for example, and the gables and the granite posts which once anchored a handsome iron fence. The 1870's in England saw the development of the Queen Anne style where many ideas were borrowed from Gothic architecture, especially the expression on the exterior of the skeleton of the buildings. Although not Queen Anne in plan, the emphasis here on tall, well-articulated chimney stacks, the half-timbered effect of the side porches, along with the vertical massing, shows the style's influence on Fassett.

Also Queen Anne in character is the profusion of materials and textures: brick, granite, sandstone, red marble, slate and iron which, with the many projections and recessions, create an effect of linear richness.

A similar comparison can be made between the Woodman Building (Cook, Everett and Pennell) and Fassett's J. B. Brown Memorial Building at 523-543 Congress Street (fig. 72), across Casco Street from Mechanic's Hall. Although the lower portion is obscured by "modern" store fronts, the upper four floors are ample evidence of Fassett's ability to handle a business block with more than ordinary success.

In the Woodman Building, horizontal rows of windows and bold unbroken stringcourses are emphasized; here the strong verticals separating the bays and the individual windows are stressed. In place of a mansard roof, the window bays are terminated on the roof line by pointed gables. As in Fassett's house, Queen Anne Gothic is also evident in the chimney stacks.

The divisions between the stories are articulated horizontally, but Fassett's use of spiny vertical elements which carry right up through the roof line gives this building a distinctive character on a narrow, curving street.

Fassett's name is linked with the western development of the business district up Congress Street. His commercial buildings

Signature in stone, Brown Building

193

194

extend from the Lancaster Building (now Loring, Short and Harmon) at Monument Square to the Baxter Building, the Congress Square Hotel and the Lafayette Hotel. His institutional buildings include the Society of Natural History, built in 1879 on Elm Street and torn down in 1971, the Portland Public Library of 1888, the Home for Aged Women on Emery Street; and in his own neighborhood, Butler School in 1879, McLellan School in 1886 and the Maine General Hospital's original wing.

In the same block as the McLellan school and within sight of his own dwelling stands Williston Church (fig. 73) at 32 Thomas Street, which Fassett began in 1877. It is one of five important churches designed by him in Portland.

The Williston Congregational Church was an offshoot of an older group, in this case the State Street Church, organized in 1873. The cornerstone of the present structure was laid in 1877 and the church was occupied for the first time the following year. Perhaps the most important historical contribution of this congregation was the formation in 1881 of the Young People's Society of Christian Endeavor. The two transept windows were given in commemoration of this event.

Although the term Gothic, as a church building style, recurs regularly in the history of architecture, each period interprets it differently. The Gothic Revival churches, both frame and masonry, of the 1840's were severely symmetrical; Fassett's assimilation of Queen Anne ideas has become more obvious.

The Queen Anne style, with its borrowings from domestic Gothic architecture, developed an open, assymmetrical and picturesque plan. In place of a strong central entrance flanked by towers, the corner site is emphasized by a strong tower. One entrance is found on the Thomas Street flank, another tucked around the corner on Carroll. Window placement and size are varied to include groups of three small windows, tall, single, narrow lances, paired openings and the broad mullioned window facing the McLellan school.

As in his own dwelling, Fassett has used a variety of materials and textures with various stones and brick both

195

74. *Edward Alling Noyes House. Stick Style, late nineteenth century*

plainly and ornamentally laid. The lean but variegated surface is in many ways much simpler than the J. B. Brown Building or the architect's dwelling at 117-119 Pine Street. However, where there may be more unbroken surfaces here, there is also a more sculptural sense in the composition of the masses.

JOHN CALVIN STEVENS I – NEW STYLES

STICK STYLE

Stick Style, though not the most poetic style name, aptly describes the house at 394 Danforth Street (fig. 74). On land bought from Horatio N. Jose (who briefly owned the former Stephen McLellan House, now the Cumberland Club) in 1870, Edward Alling Noyes had his home built sometime before 1873. Noyes was an interesting man; a banker and business leader, a city councillor responsible for Portland's first electric street lighting in 1883, and deeply involved in the arts. His house certainly suggests that he had a good eye for architecture as well as a certain amount of stylistic daring.

While builders' books, (both European and American, with engravings of plans and elevations) had been generally available since the early part of the nineteenth century, architectural periodicals first appeared in the latter half of that century. British publications, like *Builder's News,* were circulated in the late 1860's, while American publications followed about a decade later. The availability of novel architectural ideas must account for the freshness of this house which is comparable — on a much smaller scale to be sure — to rather grand English dwellings and to the avant-garde summer architecture of early Richard Morris Hunt in Newport, Rhode Island.

A mixture of medieval resonances with some fashionably rustic Swiss chalet lurks behind this unusual dwelling. The main body of the house forms a generous, spatial L. The resulting space is occupied by a broad porch extending a full bay

75. *Detail: Noyes House*

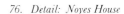

76. *Detail: Noyes House*

197

beyond the principal structure. The plan is assymetrical and free of the lateral containment of earlier styles, projecting various individual forms against the sky. The eaves project boldly from the central blocks; the gables are flattened at their apexes and crowned by finials; the thrust of the porch to the right is countered by the forward projecting window bay on the left; a narrow, shallow projecting gable marks the porch entrance which is echoed in the linear struts which bracket the principal eaves.

Besides a picturesque silhouette, informal but calculated, the sense of skeleton expressed on the outside is made obvious by the discriminating use of wood in this structure. The tall, thin members of the window bay with their cross supports, the bony articulation of the porch and the intricate bracketing of the eaves (fig. 75) suggest a structure turned inside out. The net effect, of course, is of delicate verticality which is aided by the finely worked chimney stacks played against substantial masses.

Materials, too, are important here. Not only the roof, but the siding is of slate, while the woodwork is charmingly decorative (fig. 76). Pierced stars, modified gargoyles, stars (in relief and incised), abound; balusters, a flattened lacy echo of baroque forms, open a flow of space in the porch, emphasized by the lateral lattice work.

THE SHINGLE STYLE

The terms Shingle Style and Stick Style were coined by Vincent J. Scully, Jr., who writes of John Calvin Stevens I in his 1955 book *The Shingle Style,* an offshoot of his earlier work with Antoinette Downing, *The Architectural Heritage of Newport, Rhode Island.*

Stevens began his architectural career in the office of Francis H. Fassett in 1873. In 1881, at the age of twenty-six, he was sent to Boston to manage a branch of the firm where he was constantly exposed to the latest architectural developments.

198

77. John Calvin Stevens I drawing of his residence built 1884

Stevens founded his own firm in Portland in 1884 and built a residence for his family at 52 Bowdoin Street (fig. 77), in sight of the Western Promenade and on land once part of the large J. B. Brown estate. It provided Portland with an early example of a new style which would considerably influence the aesthetics of the twentieth century.

In the Bowdoin Street residence, in the James Hopkins Smith House on Falmouth Foreside (fig. 79), and in the C. A. Brown

199

78. Stevens House today

79. *James Hopkins Smith House 1885. Falmouth Foreside, John Calvin Stevens I*

House in Delano Park, Cape Elizabeth (fig. 80 – all built within three years – Stevens worked with plans and materials dramatically different from the Stick Style house on Danforth Street.

Most obvious at first glance is the lower, broader profile of his house. In contrast to the strong vertical proportions of earlier houses, a broad low gambrel gable dominates the street façade. With its size and overhang, the first story seems low and intimate. Unlike the predictable cube of buildings of the earlier part of the century, this silhouette is open and rambling. No one façade or view summarizes the whole. Chimney stacks, smaller gables, projecting bays, recessed porches (the window bay on the left front was once the entrance porch, fig. 78) reveal the architect's vision in terms of interpenetrating masses, of nooks and crannies.

200

*80. C. A. Brown House 1886-1887. Cape
Elizabeth, John Calvin Stevens I*

It is no coincidence that the two contemporaneous dwellings by Stevens were summer or country houses, as were other Shingle Style buildings at Newport, Tuxedo Park, Bar Harbor, and Long Island. It is an informal style (even in its mansion-size examples) using informal materials. Shingles, not clapboards, above irregularly set brick or field stone with terra cotta decorative panels characterize these houses. It is a use of less refined and more natural materials. In keeping, windows are varied in size, placed assymmetrically and suggest the kind of plan where rooms are clustered and projected rather than being arranged symmetrically off a central hall.

Shingle Style architecture by its very nature is specifically residential, or domestic. The only exceptions seem to be resort casinos and yacht clubs which in any event are quasi-domestic.

81. Oxford Building 1886-1887,
John Calvin Stevens I

202

Carving around entranceway

When Stevens planned the Oxford Building in 1886-1887 (fig. 81) or the remodeling of the State Street Church façade in 1892-1893, and added the parish house to Fassett's original Williston Church in 1905, he had obviously different design and stylistic problems.

A business block, like a church structure, rarely allows itself the luxury of the informal or picturesque. But a new spirit and

203

stylistic daring certainly infused Stevens' commercial venture.

Basically a three-bay façade like the Board of Trade Building on Exchange Street, the Oxford Building at 185-187 Middle Street has a concentration of design not possible in the larger Woodman and J. B. Brown Buildings. Four stories high, with a strong central axis worked out by the arched entrance, a projecting two story bay and an echoing broad arched fourth story window, the rectangular façade is distinguished by its rich surface.

Here, as in the domestic buildings, Stevens found a variety of textures: brick, stone and terra cotta, wood and glass (the glass bricks of the lower floor are a recent modification); all ranging from smooth to rough, from refined to natural. Neatly patterned brick at the top contrasts with unfinished stone lintels and entrance surrounds. The terra cotta scrolled panels between the second and third stories are echoed in the amusing grotesques flanking the entranceway.

The deep, arched openings, much more massive in intent and effect than the more delicately profiled arches encountered heretofore, signalize a building style inspired by the Romanesque period. That pre-Gothic time before the delicacy of the pointed arch, when rhythms were horizontal and substantial, fitted nicely into the mood of the 1880's and 1890's.

THE ROMANESQUE REVIVAL

The older Francis Fassett found Stevens' new forms interesting. This is especially evident in his design for the Portland Public Library (fig. 82). Planned ten years after his Williston Church, this structure at 619 Congress Street is both more sensuous and more sculptural. Borrowing its façade freely from a Romanesque church, it suggests the nave and side aisle plan, a central high gable flanked by buttressing side sections. The deeply recessed main portal is complemented on either side by large arched windows, while above, a row of more closely-spaced arched openings leads the eye upward to a large rondel.

205

Decorative medallion and stonework

Apparently, Fassett not only worked out some new architectural ideas in the Library building, but donated his services as well and became one of the early trustees. The building was paid for by James Phinney Baxter, who became its first president.

Fassett was certainly aware of Henry Hobson Richardson's work in Boston and environs. Richardson's famous Trinity Church had been started in 1872 and his other buildings – commercial blocks, dwellings, libraries, railroad stations – had such a pervasive influence that the style is often called Richardsonian Romanesque.

206

Colonnettes of entranceway

Obviously more formal, the Portland Public Library nevertheless provided Fassett with many picturesque opportunities. Red brick, Ohio sandstone and brown freestone are combined in stripes, checks, scrolls and two round profile reliefs.

Although Romanesque Revival was a style best-suited to substantial, dependable public buildings, it found its way to private dwellings of both grand and more intimate scales. Perhaps a facile but apt phrase to describe it would be "masonry shingle style," the two styles are not only co-eval; they share much the same architectural point of view.

The dwellings at One Thomas Street and 150 Vaughan

207

83. *Harry Butler House*
    1892-1894,
    John Calvin Stevens I

84. *Richards-Ward House*
    1893,
    John Calvin Stevens I

Street were designed by John Calvin Stevens I during 1892-1893. The Thomas Street house (fig. 83) was commissioned by young Harry Butler, banker and philanthropist, the son of Moses Butler, lawyer and one-time mayor, after whom the Butler School is named.

Familiar elements from Stevens' own residence on Bowdoin Street are the assymetrical plan with its horizontal feeling, the picturesque silhouette and the importance of varied rich textures. What is different is a sense of greater weight and solidity. Certainly the thick corner tower makes this point, as do the breadth of the window openings and the heaviness of the lintels. Another Stevens' touch is evident in the broad porch's shadowy recession and the rank of three bowed windows above, balancing the bold projection of the tower; for as rich as this is in actual texture, it is equally rich in light and shade.

The house at 150 Vaughan Street (fig. 84) sits on land (part of the original Bramhall Estate) bought by Frederick E. Richards in 1892 from Philip Brown, a son of J. B. Brown. Richards, also a banker and president of Union Mutual Company, chose Portland's leading architect to design an appropriately impressive structure for his home.

Typical of Portland homes designed in the Queen Anne and Romanesque Revival styles, this one has unhappily lost the upper portion of its side-circling piazza (fig. 85). The stone remains of the piazza begin next to the entranceway and balloon out around the north corner, going under the projecting side wing.

Even lacking the upper part of this important curve, the rectangular massing that remains nicely manipulates the surrounding space. At the southern corner of the façade, there is a three story gabled projecting bay. Then comes the massive one-story entrance portico, stepped out even more. The two-bay principal block behind it is resolved into a set-back, laterally-projecting ell, once more tightly joined to the porch.

85. Original porch, Richards-Ward House

209

It is interesting to compare the Butler and Richards Houses: the latter, though larger, has much more restrained decorative detail. The flat open work of the upper portion of the portico, the neat, closely spaced brick brackets of the cornice, the handsome scroll panels flanking a side window, even the chimney stacks and the sharp edges of the gables, all suggest a direction which Stevens was to take in his architectural design.

CLASSICAL REVIVAL REDEFINED

The turn of the century saw a renewed interest in our own colonial and Federal architecture, and in Neo-Classical forms as a whole. The Philadelphia Exposition of 1876 had given Americans a chance to look back on their own history, while the Chicago Columbian Exposition of 1893 "sanctified" the Neo-Classical or Beaux-Arts tradition. Even though the Queen Anne style incorporated some classical motifs (Palladian windows, columned porticos, an occasional pediment), these remained decoration for a basically romantic, picturesquely rambling plan.

The new buildings, however, were regular and symmetrical in plan, if not pure in detail. Numerous residences in the Western Promenade area were designed in this period, many of them by Stevens and his son John Howard, who joined the firm in 1906. The Stevens firm designed the Portland Museum of Art which adjoins the McLellan-Sweat Mansion.

With the nation's awakened sense of history, dwellings like the former McLellan Mansion were becoming museum houses. Mrs. Lorenzo de Medici Sweat, its last owner, donated the McLellan House and the funds for building the adjacent galleries to the Portland Society of Art, which numbered James P. Baxter, John Calvin Stevens I, and John Howard Stevens among its presidents. The classical details of the museum both within and without are obvious. The coffered rotunda with its deep niches is particularly handsome.

During construction of the Museum, the Stevens firm also

210

took part in the building of a new City Hall, the third such building to be erected on that site since 1862.

The choice of site had not been an easy one. A proposal had been made for placing all municipal buildings (and a separate auditorium) on the remaining borders of Lincoln Park where County and Federal buildings already abutted.

Despite a widespread financial panic in 1907, Portland's progress seems to have been unaffected. The new Federal Building, like the Customs House in the early 1870's, was designed by U.S. Treasury architects. It was completed in 1911, a year after the Cumberland County Court House (fig. 86) across Pearl Street and also facing on Federal. The Court House was designed by George Burnham, a local architect important for his residential, recreational, civic and commercial buildings.

*86. Cumberland County Courthouse
1906-1910,
George Burnham*

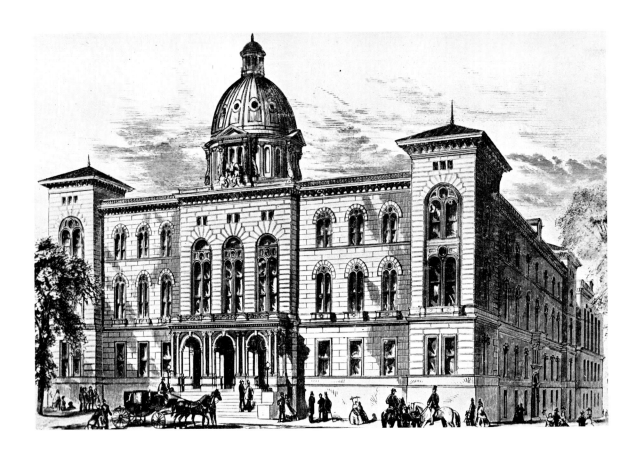

87. Old City Hall 1858-1864, burned 1866

Burnham, only thirty-one when the cornerstone was laid in 1906, reveals in this structure his solid belief in the Neo-Classical, Beaux-Arts tradition. The Court House style, like its counterpart across the street, is indubitably Federalese.

At the turn of the century, many American architects went to the Beaux-Arts School in Paris, or studied with those who had. Although the Neo-Classical tradition of adapting classical and Renaissance detail has fallen into disrepute (much as Victorian was a perjorative for so long), in the hands of an architect like Burnham, the Court House is properly impressive, handsomely proportioned, and well built from both structural and utilitarian viewpoints.

Its high basement story of large granite blocks provides a sturdy underpinning to the impressive motifs of the upper floors; the main façade is well balanced by slightly pedimented end bays, flanking a Doric colonnade. The colonnade idea is

212

88. Old City Hall rebuilt by Frances H. Fassett, burned 1908

repeated on the side elevations where massive columns and entablature project strongly to lend a sculptural effect to what could otherwise have been a dry but exact structure.

Meanwhile the city council was unwilling to make a decision on the site for the new City Hall, so the matter was put to a referendum. The traditional site won, and the fashionable New York firm of Carrère and Hastings was engaged, with the Stevens firm as the local consulting architects.

The two previous city halls, destroyed by fire in 1866 (fig. 87) and 1908 (fig. 88), had three-part entrances, crowned on the roof line by octagonal domes. Each had a central section with lateral wings and was classical in detail.

In 1905 and 1906, Carrère and Hastings had designed the House and Senate office buildings in Washington and the New York Public Library, opened to the public in 1911.

89. *City Hall 1909-1912, Carrère and Hastings*
National Register of Historic Places 1973

Carrère was particularly proud of the Portland City Hall (fig. 89). It is regrettable that he died before its completion. He had reason to be pleased with this structure. While it does not have the imaginative daring of the concurrent architecture of Louis Sullivan or Frank Lloyd Wright, it has succeeded well within its imposed stylistic limits.

Based loosely on a French Renaissance Hôtel de Ville, the City Hall design uses its classical vocabulary in a manner differing from its neighboring government buildings. The central

portion is set back and the wings project forward to form a handsome entrance court. The paving stones are set in a semi-circle leading to a broad stairway which rises above the basement story to the three arched entrances. The simple detailing of the iron grille-work gates is subtly repeated in the slender bell tower, surmounted by the sailing ship weathervane which Carrère himself designed.

The use of classical pediments, columns, balustrades and urns is familar, yet one could not confuse this structure with

215

Fore Street showing Boothby Square

Lincoln Park as it appeared in 1874

the Customs House. In contrast to the Neo-Baroque robustness of that earlier building, the City Hall has a linear refinement characteristic of a more academic taste. Yet it is large and manages beautifully to accommodate a 3,000 seat auditorium with its famous Kotszchmar Organ, in addition to the usual municipal offices and facilities. Its calculated refinement gives it the exact balance between handsomeness and solidity necessary to a city hall yet with no intimidating sense of bulkiness.

216

OPEN SPACES: SQUARES AND PARKS

Although the shape and topography of the peninsula created street patterns with handsome and changing vistas, planned parks and open spaces were not developed until late in the nineteenth century.

When the Eastern and Western Promenades were laid out in 1836, the *Eastern Argus* noted, "They may be very pleasant for those that keep horses and gig and have nothing else to do but ride about, but they will not be the least advantage to nine-tenths of the taxpayers of the city." By 1876 horse-cars were running the length of the peninsula.

During his terms as Mayor in the 1890's, James Phinney Baxter managed with great difficulty to acquire most of the land needed for the full development of these two areas. A sea view, including the eighteenth century site of Fort Allen, enlivened by the numerous islands of Casco Bay to the east, and a mountain view for the setting sun to the west, can be enjoyed. Broad parkland perimeters give the resident and visitor a relaxed and verdant change from the turbulent activity of the crowded city between.

For such a dense city, however, there is an unusual amount of open space. Lincoln Park, originally laid out after the fire as a safety measure, is a large, shady area which also offers a refreshing counterpoint to the abutting government buildings. Boothby Square, Monument Square and Longfellow Square also provide punctuation to the bustle of the city, as do the historic Eastern and Western Cemeteries.

In 1883 the Portland Soldiers and Sailors Monument Association was formed to raise funds. The Old Kimball-Clapp City Hall was removed and in 1889 the cornerstone of the monument was laid. The commission for the pedestal went to Richard Morris Hunt of New York. The sculpture commission was awarded to Franklin Simmons of Portland. The heroic bronzes, soldiers and sailors crowned by Our Lady of Victories, (fig. 90) were installed in 1891 and Market Square was then renamed Monument Square.

90. Our Lady of Victories Monument, dedicated 1891. Richard Morris Hunt and Franklin Simmons

217

91. Longfellow Monument and Square, dedicated 1888,
   Francis H. Fassett and Franklin Simmons